PENGUIN BOOKS

Forgotten Pleasures

Ruth Rudner writes: "Before I went to live in the Alps in 1963, I wrote about skiing for *Ski* magazine. After I went to live in the Alps, I wrote about Alps—skiing, hiking, climbing, *being* in the Alps. Eventually, finding myself again in America, i.e., Alpless, I began to explore American mountains—and to write about Rockies, Sierras, and Appalachians as well as Alps. I spend most of my time outdoors and have always preferred mountains to schools, although I went to a number for as long as I could bear it: Antioch College, Columbia School of General Studies, University of Vienna Summer School. Outside interests? Hiking, skiing, climbing, all the wild places of the world and especially Tibet, travel, dogs, modern dance. . . ."

Miss Rudner, who lives in New York when not in the wilderness, is also the author of *Guide to Skiing the Alps, Wandering: A Walker's Guide to the Mountain Trails of Europe, Huts and Hikes in the Dolomites,* and *Off and Walking: A Hiker's Guide to American Places.*

Forgotten Pleasures

A GUIDE FOR THE SEASONAL ADVENTURER

Ruth Rudner

With drawings by James Goldsmith

PENGUIN BOOKS

Penguin Books Ltd, Harmondsworth,
Middlesex, England
Penguin Books, 625 Madison Avenue,
New York, New York 10022, U.S.A.
Penguin Books Australia Ltd, Ringwood,
Victoria, Australia
Penguin Books Canada Limited, 2801 John Street,
Markham, Ontario, Canada L3R 1B4
Penguin Books (N.Z.) Ltd, 182–190 Wairau Road,
Auckland 10, New Zealand

First published in the United States of America in
simultaneous hardcover and paperback editions by
The Viking Press and Penguin Books 1978

LIBRARY OF CONGRESS CATALOGING IN PUBLICATION DATA
Rudner, Ruth.
Forgotten pleasures.
1. Outdoor recreation. I. Title.
GV191.6.R8 1978b 796.5 78–3686
ISBN 0 14 00.4932 0

Printed in the United States of America by
Offset Paperback Mfrs., Inc., Dallas, Pennsylvania
Set in Linotype Caslon

Acknowledgments

The information in this book comes from a lot of helpful people. My thanks to them all: Duncan Morrow, at the National Park Service in Washington; William C. Wilkinson, III, at the U.S. Department of Transportation in Washington; William E. Trout, III, of the American Canal Society; Basil Kamener, of the Skate-Sailing Association of America; Martin Luray and Art Tokle, authors of *The Complete Guide to Cross-Country Skiing and Touring;* Ilene Marckx, of the Tahoma Audubon Society; Ann Carter, Pine Barrens naturalist, for the use of her library; Stiles Thomas, for his information about hawks; Renee Lipson, Marie Winn, Stephanie Murphy, Jim Goldsmith, Natasha Herron, Anita Herron, Lucille Rhodes, Larry Rudner, Al Rudner, Leon Greenman, Walter Pratt, and Mark Twain, for a great miscellany; and my editor, Becky Singleton, whose idea, after all, this was.

For Larry

Table of Contents

Introduction

*I reckon I got to light out for the territory ahead of the rest,
because Aunt Sally she's going to adopt me and sivilize me,
and I can't stand it. I been there before.*
                                                    —Huckleberry Finn

The territory got smaller since Huck Finn's day. Civilization got bigger and getting out of its grip got harder. For sure we have been trying. By the thousands we rush headlong through forests, up mountains, into water. Any available wilderness will do. Even the sky is up for grabs.

Simple pleasures and great adventures, both a matter of course to Huckleberry Finn, have either been entirely forgotten by us, or become highly technological. Our current enthusiasm for getting back to Nature has made so great a mystique of equipment that the adventure seems nowhere near so important as the gear we must first purchase. No wonder so many glorious Sunday afternoons are spent in front of a television set! Faced with the array of equipment, the decisions to be made about it, the techniques to be learned, and, on top of it all, a lurid emphasis on danger, a darkened room and mindless box seem to offer immense safety.

But safety never yet produced that pleasure whose core is adventure. Adventure is our birthright.

It need not necessarily mean climbing Nanga Parbat. Adventure can mean, as well, grabbing a bucket and going out some lovely summer afternoon to pick berries.

Doesn't sound awfully adventurous? Well, if berrying is something you haven't done since you were a kid, or haven't ever done, and if doing it breaks your routine and gets you outside into the natural world, which is a place you don't go to at all, at least not without two hundred dollars' worth of equipment on your back, and if, in spite of all this, you just up and do it, I'd say that was adventurous.

Anyway, that's what this book is about—the adventure of grabbing a bucket and going. Any bucket. Any going. So much the better that the going depends on Nature—on the renewable, circular, never-ending seasons. In the routine of our city or suburban lives, doesn't it often seem that time speeds by so fast we can barely grasp it, hardly understand where it all went, find ourselves aware only of its loss? But Nature, with no exact routine in its very specific structure, stretches time, lengthens it, gives it to us as if it will last forever. Indeed, it will.

People who live in the country can watch the seasons ease one into the next, while city people are often surprised, when they spend a day in the country, to discover it is autumn. But there is an irony in the fact that some city dwellers seem more aware of natural things than people who have always lived in the country. City people who make the effort to go to the country, seek out silent things; they go for a walk, a ski tour on newly fallen snow, a few hours spent searching for spring greens, a horseback ride through the autumn woods. Country people, used to being able to walk out the back door and pick berries for their breakfast, often spend *their* leisure hours on snowmobiles or trail bikes. I asked some country friends about this (friends who enjoy snowmobiles *and* silent things). Their answer was that city people come to the country to get away from noise and excitement, but since country people don't have much of either, those mechanical things provide their otherwise quiet lives with thrills.

My thought then was that while many city people may have forgotten the simple pleasures primarily because they *seem* not to be easily accessible, many country people have also forgotten them just because they are too easily accessible. (How come so few people seem to know that there was fun before there were motors . . . ?)

Just outside the biggest, most densely populated cities lies the country. It is often accessible by public transportation. In some places the "country" is available inside the city. City parks and, in a number of urban areas, national parks offer wild places, of a sort.

The national parks are National Recreation Areas, under the jurisdiction of the National Park Service, Department of the Interior. By taking over the management of some parks formerly maintained by cities or privately, as well as by purchasing land, the National Park Service is attempting to preserve historic landmarks *and* insure a kind of wilderness experience for urban dwellers—not to mention the birds and animals who held the initial rights to the land.

San Francisco, Cleveland, Chicago, Michigan City, Gary, and New York City all have access to national parks via public transportation. Almost all of their systems could be better, but at least they exist.

Also located near urban areas are twenty-nine National Recreation Trails, so designated by the National Trail Systems Act of 1968. (More about national parks and trails at the end of the book.)

Fields, streams, hills, lakes, rocks, trees, are everywhere. Empty lots, city, county, state, and national parks, and privately maintained land open to the public: all are places where simple adventures—and much forgotten pleasure—are to be found.

Many owners of private property are generous about allowing their land to be used for outdoor activities. Their permission, however, should always be asked. And everything on the property—gates, trees, flowers, animals, and so forth—should be left as it was found.

Nobody's permission is required to use most public land, but it should be treated with the same respect. The landscape—however tough it appears—is fragile. Its ecological balance is easily upset. If we mean to continue indulging in the simple pleasures Nature offers, we had better leave her the means to continue offering.

Before we became so ecologically oriented, many of the pleasures in this book were simpler. But they were also, often, more wasteful, in ways the land can no longer tolerate. The impact of the sheer numbers of people who go outside makes necessary protective measures for the land, measures that sometimes seem restrictive to the people who use it. What this really means it that the simple pleasures cost us a little more effort—or ingenuity. But they are still simple, still unmechanized, still focused on natural things and on individual action.

In this book, pleasures are divided according to seasons. More or less. Obviously, in warm climates, some activities, like shell collecting, can be done year round and some, like snowshoeing, not at all. Other activities overlap seasons, although the experience of them might change radically from season to season. Of these, some have been placed in the season in which they are first done, others in the season in which they are most easily, aesthetically, or gently done. All subjective, you understand. Some may seem arbitrary. Musseling, for instance. This is a summer activity on the East Coast, but can only be done in winter on the West Coast. It is included in "Summer" because I live on the East Coast. Although it changes as much as everything else with the seasons, the night seems to me to be its own season and has been placed outside the four usual ones. Most of the activities are things I do, but some are new to me. About these I have collected information from friends. I expect to incorporate most of these new activities into my life . . . as soon as I'm finished with this book.

Each season—with the exception of "Night"—begins with a short walk in Black Rock Forest. Each season the forest becomes an entirely new place, the same walk, another walk entirely. (In this context the night differences will parallel those of the seasons by day.) Black Rock Forest, owned by Harvard University, is used by it for research in forestry. It consists of about four thousand acres that boast a dozen summits over fourteen hundred feet high and endless craggy outcroppings. A little more than an hour's drive from New York City and crossed by many paths, it is a place where one can easily walk for a day or an hour.

At the end of most of the chapters is a list of coordinate books, field guides, and other publications. You will also find there lists of clubs and various other sources of information and instruction about each subject for which such things exist. My apologies for the good books that have been left out. Only those I was personally able to investigate have been listed. Other good sources of information may also have, inadvertently, been excluded. I would be grateful to know about them all.

I have made no attempt to be scientific with either names or descriptions, since this book is not meant as a detailed guide book but as a way of presenting a few uncomplicated things to do outside. Besides, I think it's more important to see, feel, hear, smell, and taste than to name. The experience of nature is sensory, sensual. What else, after all, is pleasure?

Spring

One day the ice breaks up, the melting snow swells the beginnings of streams that pour foaming and new down the sides of mountains, transforming gentle brooks into swift rivers, paths into streams and woods into swamps—a great, wild rush of life. The sky is filled with the sound of birds; the first wildflowers spring up out of the damp forest; the backroads turn to rich, dark mud; winter-lean animals celebrate the earth's awakening; tiny new green buds burst open.

Even while city people are saying, "We don't have spring any more," the fruit trees around them are bursting extravagantly into flower while the broad-leaved trees produce their subtle blossoms. Violets and bluets poke their way up through the moist ground in city parks, and in the woodlands shy trillium appears, lady's slipper and bunchberry—eternally new, every year a surprise. The secretive woodcock jumps and spins in a clearing at dusk in his odd and marvelous courting dance. The sound of spring peepers fills the air wherever there is a pond.

A sleeping world awakes; everything on earth is born.

A Short Walk in
Black Rock Forest

In the cool morning air the sun feels especially warm as I leave Mine Hill Road and climb the path into the forest. A few patches of ice still cling to rocks on the northwest face of the steep slope, but the path itself is soft, muddy in its steepest sections. The direct, short, uphill climb evolves into a traverse high up on the hillside and, within minutes, I reach the path junction—the short Sackett Mountain Trail lies to the left, a section of the twenty-odd-mile trail from Schunemunk to Storm King to the right. I turn left. The still bare trees have the tiniest beginnings of buds. The path —cushioning, comfortable, accepting of my feet—is most welcome after the frozen, unresponsive ground of winter. So is the first open rock ledge. From here I can look out over the valley, north to the Shawangunks and beyond, to the Catskills: faint purple shadows of mountains which rise miles and miles and miles from me.

Continuing, I come to a full and rushing brook, pursuing in swirls and falls its rocky course. At its shaded edge a curtain of icicles hangs from a low branch, reaching down into the water. Idly, I break one off. It breaks easily. A few drops of water slide off the bottoms of the others. It is only a matter of days before none of them will exist. Nature so willingly lets go her creations. If I had not walked here today I would have missed this moment. Soon I come upon the ruins of a log cabin, built sixty years ago—part of the walls and a stone chimney are all that's left. Except for the sound of the stream rushing past a little below, this place is silent, empty, waiting for the people who will never come back.

Not far beyond the cabin I cross an old road, now grassed over so that it seems nothing but a broad path. On my right I find the first of the blue markers indicating the trail I want. I head up the trail, into spring in earnest. The path has become a stream. Trying to stay within the bounds of the path I step from rock to rock to twig, but the stream becomes fuller and fuller. Finally I leave it altogether, making my way higher up through bushes, saplings, still-bare trees, delighted when I come upon a large dry rock, brightened with sun since the budding trees do not yet stop its light. I climb on top of the rock to lie a few minutes in the warm noon.

Where patches of grass find clearing among the dead leaves, they are already green. Laurel, insistent, ubiquitous laurel, is a rich dark green. In a matter of weeks it will burst into pink or white flowers that will expand as far as one can see. The rock—my rock and the rock that is everywhere here, solid granite that crops out along the hillsides, on ledges, in the path itself, nestled beneath trees—is gray; and the trees—

the oak, ash, basswood, and maple, but mostly oak—
blend, without their leaves, into the gray.

I continue the short way along the blue-marked path
to another junction with the Schunemunk-Storm King
path, turn left onto it, and almost immediately come
to the short spur leading to Echo Rock. This vast, flat,
sloping rock one hundred feet above Sutherland Pond
is, for me, the jewel of the forest. It cannot be seen
from the main path. It looks out on no roads. Now and
then a plane passes by overhead, but otherwise there is
no sound but the birds and wind. The pond is deep blue
and glistening, the only natural pond in the forest. Two
ducks, who probably wintered there, swim from somewhere in the middle toward the near shore, then dis-
appear from my view. If I wanted to call out to the
hills beyond the pond I would be answered an instant
later by a resounding echo that was born with the formation of these mountains four hundred million years
ago. But I am enamored of the warm spring silence and
will not interrupt.

Southeast of me I can see Bear Mountain and beyond that, in this clear day, the towers of New York
City—a dream city, hazy at this distance, as if it were
something created out of my own mind.

I leave the rock to return to the path, now comfortable again, dry, straight, and gentle as it cuts through
thick brush. With a great flapping of wings, a grouse
flies up suddenly in front of me, then circles to some
distance behind. Walking on, I come to an oasis of
pine—a stand of red pine, a world unique in the area.
The light sifts through the high trees in awesome rays;
the smell of pine needles is already rising from the
ground, even before the summer's heat. I walk slowly

through, eager for this section of forest to last. But it is no longer than it ever was, and within minutes I cross a dirt road to begin the gentle uphill leading to the base of the 1410-foot Black Rock. Fifteen minutes from the pines and I am there, scrambling up the solid, massive granite to the top, into a fierce wind to a view of the Hudson River, the Shawangunks, and the Catskills, to a vision of endless sky. I cross to the less exposed back side of the mountain where I can be sheltered from the wind and warmed by the sun. In this aerie above the Hudson I can become king, god, master of the river. With great satisfaction I lean back against a rock to eat my lunch.

Watching the Birds Come Back

It was a long, cold winter in the Shawangunks. I had spent it in a cabin in the woods a little uphill from a small lake. "Coldest winter in thirty-five years," the people who had lived in the area for at least thirty-five years all said. As I sat by the fire contemplating spring one late-March morning, I suddenly heard the barking of a hundred dogs. I ran outside to find the sound coming from the sky. Approaching the lake from the south, spread out, high up in a great V, was a flock of Canada geese. They did not land, but continued on their way, trailed by the brass notes of their honking.

Spring. How perfect its fanfare. No trumpets or drums could ever have so triumphantly announced the presence of royalty. I stood marveling in their wake until, cold, I returned to the fire to see what else I could summon up.

Birds. Every spring several hundred different kinds make their way from wintering spots to breeding grounds. You don't have to be a bird watcher to watch them. Fascinating, magical creatures, the colors of

earth and jewels and light and night, the only beings
other than man who can imitate sounds they hear—
birds are quick, graceful, sometimes gangly, sometimes
silly paragons of energy. They are powerful, deter-
mined animals, regardless of whether they happen to
be hummingbirds or eagles. Like jewels, they have be-
guiled men always. Think how long pretty little ones
have been kept in cages to amuse and to decorate, or
how long man yearned for the flight of birds before he
found his own flight. A bird is one of the ultimate sym-
bols of life—the phoenix, who, dying, is consumed by
fire to be reborn out of his own ashes. (Can the eternal
search for the phoenix be considered bird watching?)

It is impossible to watch a bird and not be aware of
him in nature—where he is living, what he is eating,
how he is spending his time. At this moment of writing,
I am living on a beach with a pair of purple finches for
neighbors. Unlike either the phoenix or the Canada
goose, the purple finch is a singularly unspectacular
little bird. Now, in June, they spend much of their time
in a Japanese black pine tree next to the house. The
tree almost touches the table behind the dunes where I
eat. Every morning my finches are there; he perched on
the topmost branch, she on the one below. He sings and
she puts in an occasional chirp. She flies busily back and
forth carrying twigs and dried grasses and he watches.
Now and then they fly off together, return together,
perch on the next pine tree for a few minutes, and then
fly back to their own tree. I find that before I pour my
coffee I automatically look over to see what they are
about. If they are not there I miss them a little.

They are so small, and so utterly alive.

Birds migrate for food. (Some say they migrate because they enjoy a change of scene.) But basically, if in winter, ice, snow, and the natural seasons of plants or insects cause a bird's usual food to be unavailable in its preferred breeding area, it goes where food is available. It returns to the breeding area when food is again obtainable there. In the Northern Hemisphere most birds fly south in fall, reversing the routes in spring. (Occasional birds follow different routes for their spring and fall trips.) But some birds actually travel farther north in winter and others, in our western or midwestern states, fly east. Some just change altitudes.

There are four major routes in the United States— broad paths of air called flyways (and narrower designations within each)—used by migrating birds.

The Atlantic Flyway is traveled by birds from eastern Canada and New England, joined by some from the Northwest Territories and Alaska which first fly east. They all head down the Atlantic coast to the southeastern states or farther.

The Mississippi Flyway is also used by birds from eastern Canada and New England, and by some western birds as well. Western and eastern birds from the North all fly through central Canada to converge south of the Great Lakes and then follow the Mississippi Valley to the Gulf states.

The Central Flyway, east of the Rockies from Canada to the Gulf coast in Texas, is the most exact north-south route.

The Pacific Flyway is used by most birds from Alaska and western Canada.

What all these routes mean to us is that no one has to go very far from home for a view of returning birds, since at least some are bound to land somewhere in everybody's area. Some may move through quickly, simply flying over, as did my geese, or staying only a matter of hours or days. Some may stay for several weeks, some may arrive for good. (Others may never have left. Lots of traditional harbingers of spring have been around all winter. Since the popularity of bird feeders may have a lot to do with this, that puts a bit of a lid on the idea that birds go south for a change of scene.) Nevertheless, for those who do migrate, April and May are, in the northern half of the country, the months when they return. In the south, where spring comes sooner, so do the birds.

Some birds, seeking protection from daytime enemies, travel at night, filling the night sky with the sound of chirping. If you hear it—and particularly if there is a full moon—drop everything and rush outside. To see birds traveling across the moon is quite spectacular.

Day or night, weather has a lot to do with a bird's traveling. Most birds move north with a warm front and a light tail wind, although some larger birds— hawks, for instance—like a head wind which supports them as it does a kite. Soaring lazily and swooping along the sides of hills and mountains on the thermals, they need exert little or no energy (see "Kites"). People who fly gliders do the same thing, but the experience remains a bit more immediate if you happen to be a hawk.

Wildlife sanctuaries have been established at many of the most popular stopping points on the migratory routes. (Many of these stopping points became popular because they were the only places left in the area where there remained enough wild land with its accompanying food supply to provide for the birds.) They are active, exciting places to visit as the birds pass through, particularly at dawn or sundown, when most birds eat. On the other hand, a visit to a hawk sanctuary, like Hawk Mountain, Pennsylvania, can be lively all day long, especially during the fall migration (see "Watching Hawks"). There are bound to be sanctuaries near you.

A Field Guide to the Birds, Roger Tory Peterson, Houghton Mifflin Co., Boston, 1968. *The* field guide. Paper or hardcover.

Watching Birds, Roger F. Pasquier, Houghton Mifflin Co., Boston, 1977. A superb companion to any field guide. It tells about birds the way no field guide can— their physical characteristics, what they do, why. . . . Clear, well-written, and fascinating. Hardcover.

The Bird Watcher's America, Edited by Olin Sewall Pettingill, Jr., McGraw-Hill Book Co., New York, 1974. A collection of stories by forty-four naturalists, who talk about their own favorite places for watching birds. Personal, full of the spirit of place, it contains some of the best nature writing I've read. Hardcover.

Bird Watching with Roger Tory Peterson is written for children but is a good primer for anyone beginning to look at birds. One copy is free from: National Wildlife Federation, 1412 Sixteenth Street, N.W. Washington, D.C. 20036.

The Audubon Society Field Guide to North American Birds: Eastern Region, Alfred A. Knopf, New York, 1977. Covers the Atlantic coast to Texas and the Rockies, with full-color photographs to identify the birds; the photos are arranged according to the color and shape of the birds. Pocket size, flexible cover.

The Audubon Society Field Guide to North American Birds: Western Region, Alfred A. Knopf, New York, 1977. Same thing, but covers birds from the Rockies to the Pacific Coast.

Bird Sanctuaries

The National Audubon Society operates sanctuaries in: Alabama, California, Colorado, Connecticut, Florida, Kentucky, Louisiana, Maine, Maryland, Nebraska, Nevada, Minnesota, New York, Pennsylvania, Ohio, South Carolina, Texas, and Wisconsin. Many are open regularly to the public. At some, visiting must be arranged in advance. A few are closed to all visiting, either because any human presence would be a harmful disturbance—as, for instance, in the case of nesting areas—or because of physical inaccessibility. A free listing of these sanctuaries with a brief description of each is available from: National Audubon Society, 950 Third Avenue, New York, N.Y. 10022.

Other sanctuaries are owned and operated independently by local Audubon chapters. For information, check your phone book for a chapter near you.

Still other sanctuaries are maintained by the Fish and Wildlife Service, U.S. Department of the Interior, Washington, D.C. 20240. Regional offices will supply you with maps of the refuges in your area, descriptive brochures, and bird, animal, and reptile checklists. The seven regions are as follows:

Region 1—the West Coast; from Canada to Mexico as far east as the eastern border of Idaho, Nevada, and California. Write: Fish and Wildlife Service, U.S. Department of the Interior, Box 3737, Portland, Oreg. 97208.

Region 2—the Southwest; from Arizona through Texas and north through Oklahoma. Write: Box 1306, Albuquerque, N.M. 87103.

Region 3—the Midwest; Minnesota, Wisconsin, Michigan, Illinois, Indiana, and Ohio. Write: Federal Building, Ft. Snelling, Twin Cities, Minn. 55111.

Region 4—the Southeast; from Arkansas and Louisiana east to the coast and north to include Kentucky and North Carolina. Write: 17 Executive Pk. Dr. N.E., Atlanta, Ga. 30329.

Region 5—the Northeast; from Virginia on up. Write: U.S. Post Office and Courthouse, Boston, Mass. 02109.

Region 6—the Rocky Mountain and Plains states; from Utah, Wyoming, and Montana east to Iowa and Missouri. Write: Box 25486, Denver Federal Center, Denver, Colo. 80225.

Region 7—Alaska. Write: 813 D Street, Anchorage, Alaska 99501.

There are other places to see birds besides sanctuaries, places private people know about from their own experience. A number of people have volunteered to share that experience with strangers, allowing their names and addresses to be listed in a *Nature Guide* published by the Tahoma Audubon Society; they can be contacted to act as guides, or to provide information to birders or nature enthusiasts traveling in their region. The *Guide* itself, superbly conceived and carefully executed, is available for $1.30 from: *Nature Guide,* 34915 4th Avenue South, Federal Way, Wash. 98002.

The *Guide* also contains a listing of Nature Centers in the United States and Canada, excerpted from *The Directory of Nature Centers* (available for $3.00 from the National Audubon Society) and lists some additional birding places.

A Lunch of Spring

We gathered a cornucopia of food one spring morning in an area of less than a quarter mile. It was no special food preserve in which we foraged, but simply a yard, and beyond it a small field and a narrow strip of woods. Free food is everywhere. My jogging route in Riverside Park in New York is lined with shepherd's purse and chives and probably fifty other things I don't recognize. Daily I see women on the hillsides there, gathering greens into large bags and baskets. That's all you need, except a willingness to bend over and pick, a good field guide and maybe a good book of recipes for wild food.

We had not even crossed the broad lawn in front of the wisteria-draped house when we began gathering our lunch. (Actually, we were just out the front door when someone suggested eating the wisteria.) The dandelion leaves were still tender enough—and, as is the wont of dandelions, plentiful. I'm sure the lawn's owner would have been delighted to have us dig up the roots, which can be baked and ground to use as a coffee substitute, but we just took the leaves.

When we had dandelion greens enough we concentrated on plantain, a weed that follows people, simply growing wherever we walk. (Indians used to find other people's trails by keeping their eyes on the plantain.) We passed a huge old black cherry tree, just in flower. Nothing for us there until late summer, when, if we have not succumbed to utter torpor, we can pick the cherries for wine or jelly or, as the early colonists did, drop them into rum as a flavoring—if we have any rum left by late summer.

Toward the edge of the lawn we found dock and picked a bunch of the smallest, most tender leaves. (The big ones can be stuffed like cabbage, but we were no more up to that than to making coffee.) Nearby we found chives. My feeling is that there is nothing in the world, except possibly chocolate mousse, that is not improved by either onion—of which chives are one of many varieties—or garlic, an onion relative. Onion grows everywhere—in moist shady places and in dry, open ones. Everything that smells like onion is edible, although I have been told one should eat only the bulb and white parts. The green parts are supposed to absorb pollutants from the air. In spring the bulb is easy to get. The yielding soil lets go with no fight if you just hold on to the green and pull straight up. (Later on you might need a small tool to dig the bulb out.)

Not far from the chives we found lamb's quarter, one of the most common of wild foods, and a patch of milkweed. The young shoots and leaves of milkweed are a very adaptable vegetable, but since some milkweeds contain undesirable toxins, we left them to serve the monarch butterflies that should be arriving any day. The butterflies not only don't care about the toxins, they can't even manage life without milkweeds! We did take lamb's quarter, though, and a few early red clovers. Clover—red, yellow or white—is a lovely sweet thing just to nibble. It's perfectly understandable that bumblebees and cows are so enamored of it. (Once I drank fresh, rich milk, still warm from a cow pastured in a field of clover. So strong was the sweet taste of clover that it was like drinking in the whole meadow.) All clover is edible and supposedly high in protein. You can eat blossoms, leaves, and roots, and the blossoms look quite charming in a salad.

Next we came upon some wild lettuce, a relative of dandelions, but more bitter. Lettuce is supposed to make you sleepy. Whatever soporific is in it is referred to, unscientifically, as lettuce opium. But I guess you'd have to eat an awful lot. I have never, for instance, come across a warning anywhere that says, "If you eat lettuce, don't drive."

Our salad fairly complete, we gathered some garlic mustard, a member of the mustard family that smells like garlic, and can be used like it.

By now the lawn had given way to fields; a path wandered through the middle of one on its downhill way toward the woods. There had once been some digging a little way off the path, and here we came upon scraggly gray twigs scattered about—a spot to dig for Jerusalem artichokes. The gray, broken twigs are last year's dried stalks and nicely mark the spot to gather this year's crop growing beneath them. Later on the new stalks will blossom into miniature sunflowers. Jerusalem artichokes, expensive in stores if

you can find them, are common in places where the
land has once been dug up—along fences, around new
houses, landfill areas, cornfields, and so forth. They
can be gathered in fall as well as in spring and should
be ignored only in summer when they are soft, starchy,
and less nutritious.

We passed a wonderful old basswood tree, whose
sweet, chocolaty flowers can be dried to make a tea
with a chocolate flavor—ideal if you think you should
be drinking tea but would rather have chocolate. There
were a few blossoms but we didn't disturb them.
Nearby we picked some mint.

Lining the path in the woods was shepherd's purse,
another mustard plant, whose name comes from the
fact that its seedpods look like little purses. Crushed,
they add a peppery taste to salad. We threw some into
the spice bag. Then we picked some winter cress, yet
another—and very piquant—mustard; their leaves are
too bitter to use much. (Winter cress can be picked
all winter if you can find it beneath the snow. Always
bitter, it is less so before the first flower stems appear
in the spring.) Nestled low on the ground, but brilliant in their velvety darkness, were violets. Rich in
vitamin C, their appeal for me is the singular aesthetic
touch they give a salad. (Dried and candied, they are
used to decorate cakes and can be purchased for a
relatively outrageous amount in gourmet stores.)

We picked a few slender twigs from a black birch.
Steeped in hot water, it makes a lovely tea with a
wintergreen flavor. (Yellow birch does too—there just
didn't happen to be any there.) You can smell the
wintergreen just by scraping your fingernail on the
bark.

Back at the house we made our salad of dandelion greens, plantain, lamb's quarter, wild lettuce, winter cress, mustard garlic, chives, shepherd's purse, clover, and violets; we fried some bacon, threw in the dock to steam, boiled the Jerusalem artichokes and half smothered them in butter, steeped the black birch in a big pot, made some juleps to go with the mint, added a fresh loaf of home-baked bread with sweet butter— and decided living off the land was highly satisfying. Someone suggested we should have added a squirrel or two, but I didn't feel the lack.

There are two things to be mindful of when foraging. One is that many good food plants love the open areas along highways, but those that grow there have been absorbing exhaust fumes since they first bore leaves. Besides, wouldn't it be nice to get a little distance between you and your car? At least far enough back from the road that you no longer see dust on the leaves.

The other is that some plants are poisonous. The fact that an animal eats some delicious-looking plant or berry does not mean it is safe for people. Even the *test* recommended in many survival books for determining whether or not something is safe for people is unsafe for people. It suggests you chew a small mouthful of something that looks edible, holding it in your mouth. If it seems bitter, sharp, or otherwise distasteful, spit it out. If it tastes good, swallow a little of the juice, spit out the rest, and wait about eight hours. If after this you have neither become ill nor died, you repeat the test, swallowing a bit more and waiting another eight hours. In the meantime, of course, you can't eat anything else because if you got sick, how would you know for sure what caused it? The problem is that some plants, like water hemlock, contain a poison so deadly that the tiniest taste, even if spit out immediately, is likely to kill. Other poisons —small amounts acting in a short time—can cause your lips and tongue to become so swollen you cannot breathe.

Take only those things of which you are absolutely certain.

If you are certain of nothing and feel insecure even with a guide book to edible plants in your hand, try to spend a few hours with someone who knows wild foods. If you don't personally know someone, take advantage of the uncomplicated courses on edible wild foods offered by museums, botanical societies, and park departments. Check with any near you. A few hours spent foraging will show you how easily you can spend endless future hours outside without ever feeling guilty about not having done anything about dinner.

Field Guide to Edible Wild Plants, Bradford Angier, Stackpole Books, Cameron & Kelker Sts., Harrisburg, Pa. 17015, 1974. Beautifully illustrated, clear, and useful. Paper.

Edible Wild Plants of Eastern North America, Merritt L. Fernald and A. C. Kinsey, Harper & Row, New York, 1958.

Why Wild Edibles? The Joys of Finding, Fixing and Tasting—West of the Rockies, Russ Mohney, Pacific Search, 715 Harrison St., Seattle, Wash. 98109, 1975. This is a friendly book that identifies wild foods with both photos and drawings and contains a few recipes for each. Paper.

The Wild Food Trailguide, Alan Hall, Holt, Rinehart & Winston, New York, 1976. An easy-to-use guide that is also easy to carry in a pocket or pack. Paper.

Stalking the Wild Asparagus, Euell Gibbons, David McKay, New York, 1970. Paper.

Stalking the Healthful Herbs, Euell Gibbons, David McKay, New York, 1970. Paper.

The Euell Gibbons books are classics—superb for how to know and where to find and what to do with a lot of wild foods, but you may still want to carry a field guide for identification purposes.

Foraging for Dinner: Collecting Wild Foods, Helen Ross Russell, Thomas Nelson, New York, 1975. Hardcover.

Poisonous Plants of the United States and Canada, John M. Kingsbury, Prentice-Hall, Englewood Cliffs, N.J., 1964. Most guides touch on poisonous plants. This is *the* authority. Hardcover.

Deadly Harvest, John M. Kingsbury, Holt, Rinehart & Winston, New York, 1965. A smaller, less technical book on the subject. Paper.

There are a great many other good guides as well. Some are regional and available in local bookstores.

Kites

The March winds bring kites... flat kites, bowed, box, and compound kites, parafoils, and delta kites. Small children, aeronautical engineers, and everybody in between flock to the open fields and beaches to raise bats, fishes, and eagles into the sky. Ready to master the air from the earth, they eagerly lift their kites to the wind, as men have done for twenty-five centuries.

I remember running with my kite as a child to get it aloft. It rarely got there. Running is about as inefficient a way to launch a kite as there is. The proper way is to stand still, offer your kite, and hope there is enough wind—but not too much wind—to take it. If that doesn't work, try a winch launch. Hold the kite at arm's length and let it go, giving it a little line as it sinks, quickly reeling in a little line—to make it taut again—just before the kite reaches the ground. Suddenly the kite ascends, reaches the end of its line, sinks again. Let it, repeating the whole process—giving it more line and reeling it in before it touches—

any number of times until the kite gains sufficient altitude to catch a breeze that will hold it up.

Ground affects the wind. Even a light breeze, which is what you usually want, is apt to produce turbulent air over uneven ground. Trees and buildings count as uneven ground. Meadows and beaches are ideal for kite flying.

Wind, of course, is what flying kites is all about. March is the traditional kite-flying month because the vernal equinox gives rise to some very special winds. Different kinds of kites use the wind differently. The most spectacular use of the wind belongs to the stunters, which can be made to do figure eights, spins, loops, hedgehopping. These kites can also be flown in a variety of wind speeds, although they work best with a strong wind. Every kite has its own range of tolerable wind speeds: Paper kites can handle winds from about three to seven miles per hour; plastic, from eight to twelve miles per hour; heavy plastic and light cloth, from thirteen to eighteen miles per hour; sturdy cloth, from nineteen to twenty-four miles per hour.

You can gauge the wind according to a system devised in 1806 by Admiral Sir Francis Beaufort of the British Navy. Winds of one to seven miles per hour are considered "light."

Up to one mile per hour—calm; smoke rises vertically.

One to three miles per hour—smoke drifts lazily. (If you haven't got a chimney to watch, a cigarette should do. If you haven't got a cigarette, perhaps you have a friend with one?)

Four to seven miles per hour—leaves rustle.

Winds of eight to twelve miles per hour are considered "gentle." Leaves and small twigs will move.

A "moderate" wind ranges from thirteen to eighteen miles per hour and causes dust to rise and small branches to move.

Winds of nineteen to twenty-four miles per hour are called "fresh." They sway trees and can break kite strings.

A "strong" wind is faster still—from twenty-five to thirty-one miles per hour. Large branches move and flying is risky, although good for stunters.

(If none of these signs is obvious to you, but the kite is behaving erratically—spinning, diving, crashing —the wind is probably too strong.)

Flying is also risky when a storm is on the way, or in rain. You can make yourself into a lightning rod then—as in Ben Franklin's experiment, for instance. You should also stay away from power lines. If your kite should somehow catch on one, let go and forget about the kite unless it frees itself. Flying a kite near airports or ground traffic, where it can be distracting to pilots or drivers, is both risky and bad form.

One of the glories of kite flying is riding the thermals—something kite flyers can share with hawks. (There are, in fact, hawks called kites, mostly in our southern states, and the earliest man-made kites were shaped like birds.) Thermals develop when a cool morning temperature gives way to a hot day. As the ground gets warm, rings of warm air rise. Air is sucked into the ring of heat from below; it rises, cools, then falls away from the ring.

Thermals also form when cool air beneath a cloud spirals downwards, disturbing the warm air below, which then rises like a tube around the column of cold air. On a warm day with a little wind, thermals are everywhere. They gain in speed as they rise. To let your kite ride, you have to get it high enough in the thermal for the current to affect it. Then it can soar and spiral on its own ... until, of course, a breeze knocks the thermal away, removing the kite's support and causing the kite to drop suddenly. Hawks, on the other hand, simply move on to the next thermal.

Kites run the gamut, from child's toy to work of art. They are virtually universal—they were flown by the Chinese in 1000 B.C. as well as by children in eighteenth-century Europe. Under the influence of kite flying, one particularly imaginative Chinese emperor ordered his prisoners, harnessed to large bamboo mats, to jump from a tower. If they survived, they were free. Kites, in fact, have from their beginning been used to lift men—either strapped to the kite itself, or lifted beneath the kite. Hang gliding, it seems, is hardly new. Kites have also been used to lift bricks to build towers, to lift jeeps, television aerials, and probably almost everything else. They have been used (and still are) for fishing and fighting. In Japan a single fighting kite in the sky is considered an invitation to a duel. The history of kites documents man's attempts to fly. As aircraft they mark the beginning of the science of aviation. But as a part of man's dream to touch the sky, they are a manifestation of his magical soul.

Their current renaissance is well tended by an international kite-flying association that publishes a quarterly magazine. There are kite-flying contests and displays, and shops devoted entirely to the art, lore, and practicalities of kite flying; in these you will find advice, as well as kites for every purpose.

Yesterday I saw a very old man on the beach. He was seated facing the sea, holding the winding reel of a kite in his hand. The kite soared high above and behind him. After a while he got up and began to walk his kite down the beach. The kite remained aloft and the old man continued to ignore it, yet held it securely. They seemed well used to one another.

The Penguin Book of Kites, David Pelham, Penguin Books, New York, 1976. A handsome, well-written, highly informative, and very charming book that contains a history of kites, plans for building them, all the science one needs for flying them, and a list of material suppliers and kite shops. Paper.

How To Make and Fly Kites, Eve Barwell and Conrad Bailey, Van Nostrand Reinhold Co., New York. Clear and simple. Hardcover.

Kite Craft: The History and Processes of Kite Making Throughout the World, Lee S. Newman and J. H. Newman, Crown Publishers, Inc., New York, 1974. A compilation of 350 photos, 84 drawings, and 18 color plates. Oversized paperback.

25 Kites That Fly, Leslie L. Hunt, Dover Publications, Inc., New York, 1971. Paper.

Kites!, Jean-Paul Mouvier, Franklin Watts Inc., New York. Paper.

Kite Tales, a quarterly magazine, published by the American Kiteflyers Association (see below).

Associations

American Kiteflyers Association, P.O. Box 1511, Silver City, N. Mex. 88061.

Maryland Kite Society, 7106 Campfield Road, Baltimore, Md. 21207.

U.S. Hang Gliding Association, P.O. Box 66306, Los Angeles, Calif. 90066.

Rock Hunting

Everybody has a landscape that makes them happiest
—forest, prairie, mountains, sea ... Mine is rock. I
like the way it looks and the way it feels. I like it as
well whether it is the Grand Teton or the little frag-
ment of the Dolomites I wear in a ring. When I hike,
my pack gets heavier and heavier with bits of rock I
find lying, sparkling, in the path, until at some inevit-
able point in every hike, I abandon all but one or two
of the smallest and prettiest. A proper rock hound,
of course, would never abandon the rocks. The hike,
maybe, but not the rocks.

Obviously, rock hunting is something to do when
one does not have to walk too far afterward with one's
treasures. This is not too difficult a requirement since
rocks are everywhere ... which also means that the
search for them can provide an outing for a person of
any temperament. You can find them in excavation sites,
on roads, or on top of 14,000-foot mountains; on sandy
beaches and riverbanks, in gorges, canyons, and stony
stream beds—dry or filled; on eroded hillsides or

rocky outcrops in fields and pastures; in areas once covered by glaciers, along exposed cliffs and talus slopes (the rock-debris slopes below cliffs and mountains); in abandoned quarries and quarry dumps; in deserts and forests and on the moon or in your backyard.

The kind of rock you will find and the minerals it will contain depend on where you look. It is the minerals that give the rock its special character or value. Rocks are composed of one mineral or several mixed together. Two rocks composed of the same minerals may be entirely different just because the percentage of each mineral in them differs. Diamonds, sapphires, rubies, and emeralds are crystals formed from minerals. In other words, just rocks. Rare, but rocks—pieces of the earth, nonetheless. Semiprecious gems like amethysts, opals, and garnets are less rare. You may well come across some, or fragments of some. (That piece of the Dolomites in my ring is a lovely amethyst found by a friend.)

The best time for rock hunting is on a clear day just after a heavy rain. The rain will have nicely washed the dust away from all exposed rock surfaces, making it possible for you to see more clearly and immediately. That same rain may have washed sand or clay away from a stream bank or a hill, exposing— for the first time—a new batch of minerals. Light also makes a tremendous difference in whether or not you find some extraordinary rock. For instance, a cliff wall with a western exposure is in deep shade in the morning, but it is fully lit in the afternoon, when the sun seeks out colors and the edges of crystals, revealing them to you in all their glory. *That* is a cliff to investigate in the afternoon. A horizontal ledge on a rise facing south will cast a shadow on the rock beneath it when the sun is directly overhead. But the slanting rays of early morning or late afternoon sun will reach under it to display everything.

The easiest places for your first hunts are areas of road or building construction and abandoned quarries and quarry dumps: places where the rock is already blasted and you can see what's inside. In the interest of good will—not to mention not being chased away—stay near the boundaries of construction sites so you don't mess up the work. As for quarry dumps, ask permission of the watchman. The one place to stay out of, *always,* is an abandoned mine shaft. It would be a shame to be trapped in one just at the beginning of a new enthusiasm.

Wherever you are hunting, walk around the area to see what is accessible. Look low and high. You may find something simply lying on the ground. If you find something high—and you want it—you will have to climb. Keep your eye out for quartz, mica, and feldspar in rock formations. These minerals you will recognize even if you *think* you've never looked at a rock before, and they are indications that there may be other rocks nearby. Quartz, with the glassy luster of its crystals, is the most common mineral on earth. Feldspar (actually the name of a group of related minerals) can easily be confused with quartz—which is OK for your purposes. (You can learn to identify the separate feldspars if you get more involved.) Mica, made up of those thinner-than-paper sheets of rock pressed together that are so pleasant just to peel apart idly, is usually recognized by everyone. Obviously these minerals are all more complex than the descriptions I've given. But every book on rocks and minerals goes into the complexities.

Rock hunting is something you can do with just a few free hours. A morning's outing to some easily accessible place is the perfect way to investigate whether you are or are *not* interested in rocks. Take along a lunch, do a little searching, then find yourself a spot for a picnic—and a chance to look over what you've found.

Once hooked, you might want to spend time scouting places that seem likely spots to hunt—some other time. This is even better than spending time rock hunting since you won't have to carry either tools or rocks.

About tools. Eventually you may acquire some specifically designed for rocks. Even from the beginning a few will make it easier if you plan to do more than just pick up the pretty pebbles in your path. But you can use tools you probably already have. A hammer with a hard steel head and handle (cast iron breaks easily when hitting rock) is useful for breaking open pieces of rock you suspect contain treasures inside. You do not need a geologist's hammer with its flat head on one side and pick on the other to begin with, but if you are going to *buy* a hammer especially, you might as well get that kind. A six-inch or eight-inch cold-steel chisel is helpful for prying crystals out of cracks in the rocks. A pocket knife can be used for digging small fossils or crystals out of soft rocks. Goggles, to protect your eyes from flying chips, are essential if you plan to do even the slightest amount of hammering. Cheap cotton gloves help protect delicate skin. Wear comfortable old clothes in which you can easily bend, climb, and kneel. (Rock hunters often sew leather patches on the knees of their jeans because they spend so much time on their knees.) Sneakers will do, but sturdy lug-soled boots will make it easier if you have any climbing to do to reach your rock and will give you better support for just wandering over rocky ground. Take something in which you can carry your finds home, and pack them carefully: all rocks should be wrapped individually in newspaper, and crystals should first be protected in pieces of cotton.

Once you find yourself leaving the road or building excavations for forays into slightly more remote places, a map of the area is a good idea. It will show you the landscape (which you can learn to read—see "Orienteering"), help keep you from getting lost, and provide a place to mark both your route to your own particular finds and their locations. United States Geological Survey maps are a great help (see end of chapter). Local maps from a rock shop in the area—if there is one—will probably be less accurate but more specific, since they will show trails, locations of good rock-hunting areas, and so forth. In the same shops you will also find whatever guides to local areas there are. The people in the shop will be knowledgeable and helpful about local rocks. If you are carrying a compass, you can use it not only to avoid getting lost, but also to determine whether a mineral you have found is magnetic or not.

If you want to keep track of the rocks you find, stick half-inch adhesive or masking tape, cut in 3/4-inch lengths, on a piece of wax paper and number each with a marker before you set out. Fold the whole thing up and put it in your pack. Take a small notebook to make notes on what you've collected and where it was. When you find a rock, just stick a number on it and number the note about it in your notebook correspondingly. Later you can use a guidebook to identify your find.

But nothing says that a rock has to be named to be enjoyed. Or that it has to be dug out of the earth or carried home. Everyone is not, by nature, a collector. The pleasure I get from the rocks I pick up along the path is highest at the moment of discovery. And I prefer being where the rocks are to taking them where I am going. I would like sometime to be in one of those phenomenal places I hear about where someone has turned over an innocuous-looking rock to find underneath—gleaming like the treasure horde of some immensely successful pirate or the richest of kings— enormous crystals of purple, rose, yellow, and gold, clear crystals and deep reds and every shade of green, the light bouncing, glancing, dazzling, off their edges, embedded every which way in the rock or lying loose and scattered in the depression beneath the rock, sparkling in this first admitted light.

I would like very much to see them, but I'm not sure I'd care about their names.

A Field Guide to Rocks and Minerals, Frederick H. Pough, Houghton Mifflin Co., Boston, 1976. Paper or hardcover.

Field Book of Common Rocks and Minerals, Frederic B. Loomis, G. P. Putnam's Sons, New York, 1948. Hardcover.

The Rock-Hunter's Field Manual, D. K. Fritzen, Harper & Row, New York, 1959.

Rocks and Minerals, Herbert S. Zim and Paul R. Shaffer, Golden Press, New York, 1957.

How to Know the Minerals and Rocks, Richard M. Pearl, McGraw-Hill Book Co., New York, 1955.

Prospecting for Gemstones and Minerals, John Sinkankas, Van Nostrand Reinhold Co., New York, 1970. Considered one of the best books on rock hunting. Clear, easy to read, it contains much useful information beyond the main text, such as the addresses of government organizations that supply geologic information and the locations of reference libraries with particularly good geological literature in all fifty states and Canada. Hardcover.

Handbook of Crystal and Mineral Collecting, William B. Sanborn, Gembooks, Menlo Park, Calif., 1966. This book concentrates on collecting rather than personally finding, gathering, and identifying.

The magazines that follow all contain advertisements for field guides for general and specific collecting sites. You may find other, local field guides in your natural history museum, in some outdoor stores in good rock-hunting regions, and in rock shops.

Gems & Minerals, P.O. Box 687, Mentone, Calif. 92359. The official magazine of the California Federation of Mineralogical Societies.

Lapidary Journal, P.O. Box 2369, San Diego, Calif. 92112. Their April issue is probably the most useful for a beginning—or not beginning—rock hunter. Called *The Rockhound Buyer's Guide,* it lists all rock-hunting clubs in the country, as well as the equipment dealers.

Rocks & Minerals, Box 29, Peekskill, N.Y. 10566. The official magazine of the Eastern Federation of Mineralogical and Lapidary Societies.

Rocks & Minerals in Canada, Box 550, Campbellford, Ontario.

A list of pamphlets and circulars describing rock and mineral locations throughout the United States is available free from: Superintendent of Documents, U.S. Government Printing Office, Washington, D.C. 20402. Ask for PL 15.

Also free: Indexes showing available U.S. Geological Survey maps for each state, and a booklet describing topographic maps. From: U.S. Geological Survey Distribution Section, 1200 South Eads Street, Arlington, Va. 22202, for areas east of the Mississippi; or from: U.S. Geological Survey Distribution Section, Federal Center, Denver, Colo. 80225, for areas west of the Mississippi.

Prices are listed in the indexes, as are instructions for ordering maps. A single order combining maps from both the East and West may be placed with one Section. In each state's index there are also lists of map reference libraries and commercial map dealers. Commercial dealers set their own prices for maps, always a bit higher than prices for maps ordered through the Distribution Sections.

Collections

Universities and natural history museums often have rock and mineral collections that you may use for reference. But you might like to have your own. Inexpensive reference collections—small specimens of common rocks and minerals—are available through natural history museums and some rock shops and mineral dealers. If you can find none of these near you, you can write for catalogs from the following:

Ward's Natural Science Establishment, P.O. Box 1712, Rochester, N.Y. 14603 and P.O. Box 1749, Monterey, Calif. 93940.

Schortmann's Minerals, 6 McKinley Avenue, Easthampton, Mass. 01027.

The Prospector's Shop, 201 West San Francisco Street, Santa Fe, N. Mex. 87501.

Odoms, Star Route A, Box 32C, Austin, Tex. 78710.

Scott Scientific, Inc., P.O. Box 2121, Fort Collins, Colo. 80521.

If you have a chance to visit the spectacular Hall of Minerals and Gems in New York City's Museum of Natural History (Central Park West at 79th Street), you will probably end up a confirmed rock hound for life. Either that, or a jewel thief.

Canoeing

It is a very small lake. Bear, moose, wolves, fisher, and fox live in the dense evergreen forest surrounding it. But they were all too shy in this early afternoon for us to have a glimpse of them as we paddled straight across the lake. It was easy paddling: no wind, calm water. A loon floating at the far end waited until we were almost upon him before taking off— flying all gangly and hunchbacked, circling around to the opposite end of the lake where we had started. He settled once again in the water. Nothing else happened except that the sun danced, sparkling, on the water.

We had portaged into the small lake, which eases— at the end toward which we headed—into a stream connecting with an enormous lake. We paddled up the clear, brown, slow stream. One end of an occasional submerged log poked its way up from the bottom. There was only the slightest of breezes on the stream, and the sun seemed hotter than it had on the small lake, almost as if this were a different season. We were three canoes and six people, all now engaged in paddling and in silence. The water flapped against the paddles. A fly buzzed.

We were hardly out of the stream when the big lake hit us full force. Rough, always rough, and miles across, it whipped into us with a wind that set us almost whirling into waves that seemed to come from two directions at once, waves and wind combining to throw us out toward the lake's raw and open center. We turned the bows into the wind, climbing each wave, being lifted by it, sliding down the backside into the trough and—finally—maneuvered the canoes a little out of the sway of the wind and close in to the bay-edged shore. We entered one of the bays. The water was as suddenly calm as it had been abruptly wild on the lake. We paddled toward the widest stretch of beach, swung the canoes around parallel to it, jumped into the water, and eased them up, high enough to be out of the reach of any errant waves. We unloaded, turned the canoes over on their sides, and set up camp at the top of the beach, where the forest came down to join it.

We did not carry tents. Two nights earlier we had had to rig a shelter with the canoes and tarps to keep from getting drenched in a sudden, violent storm. We were dry, if a bit crowded. Not carrying tents made the portages easier, I guess. It would have been considered a tremendously optimistic thing to do there, in Ontario's Algonquin Provincial Park (or in any part of the northern canoe country—Minnesota, Maine, Ontario), if we had traveled without tents deliberately. But it simply hadn't occurred to us to bring any, and we had been canoeing there for years. (What could be more proof that, not so very long ago, even a wilderness trip was less complicated. You don't have a tent? You don't use a tent.)

Setting up camp consisted mainly of choosing sites to sleep—done with an eye toward getting under the canoes fast in case of another storm. We gathered wood enough for the fire to last for hours. It was early in the season and the late afternoon had a chill to it. Night there always does. By the time dinner was over it was dark and the loons had begun their quavering cry. *That* is a sound to feel.

There are relatively few loons on the Delaware—a popular canoeing river that flows through New York, Pennsylvania, and New Jersey—but that doesn't seem to affect the people who canoe there, or on any of the myriad other loonless lakes and rivers of the United States. The absence of loons should not affect your trying out this particular pleasure—which can be either as gentle or as wild as you like.

Often you can have it both ways—albeit at different seasons—on the same stretch of river. Water that is fast during the spring run-off can be placid in summer. Sometimes the spring run-off provides whitewater possibilities on streams so tame in summer that there isn't even enough water for a canoe. Other water, in areas like Florida where it can be too hot and buggy in summer, is idyllic in spring and fall—clear, quiet, its mere existence an invitation to drift . . .

If you have never been in a canoe, make sure it *is* placid water—spring, summer or fall—you choose for learning. Whitewater canoeing comes *after* you know about canoes.

Flat-water canoeing is not difficult and canoes are

not dangerous. Even someone who has never been in one can spend a superb afternoon drifting gently down some lovely river or along the shores of a pretty lake. If you are not concentrating on rapids, you are free to concentrate on everything else : a deer that comes down to the shore to drink; an otter sliding through the water; a turtle poking its head up out of the water; on southern rivers an alligator or two; cattle grazing contentedly on the river bank; moss-covered trees, or extravagant willows dipping down into the water, forming cool, secret little chambers behind their weeping limbs; high banks that enclose you for a moment in your river, as if there were in the world only you and it; a setting sun blazing down the edge of your lake; the sound of your paddle in the silence of the world.

You can rent a canoe inexpensively almost anywhere that's close to something canoeable. And that, too, is just about anywhere. Canoes can be rented by the hour, day, week, month. Canoe outfitters can provide you with both canoe and camping equipment, if a long trip or overnight trip interests you. Many of them will arrange to transport you and the canoe to a starting point upstream or to pick you up at an end-point downstream.

Choose a calm and pretty day for your first time. Calm, because the most difficult thing you'll *ever* have to contend with in a canoe is wind. Ask the person at the canoe rental to show you how to get in and out of the canoe (a simple and, contrary to reputation, not risky act) and the basic strokes. If you can manage to make this first outing on a weekday rather than a weekend, the canoe renter will have more time to explain things to you. (I think it's a legitimate reason for taking a day off from work.) Assuming there are two of you, put the physically stronger in the stern and the quicker of vision in the bow. The canoeist in the stern is, traditionally, the captain and is most in actual, physical control of what the canoe is doing at any moment. The canoeist in front is supposed to look out for such things as submerged stumps, trees, rocks, and alligators, and announce their presence in time to turn the canoe away from a collision. If there's no such time, the paddle can be used to push away from the object, but this should be done sparingly since it frays the paddle's blade. With experience (and a little instruction) come strokes for the bowman which are designed to stave off collisions. Don't worry about those strokes first time out in a quiet place.

Wherever you are on this first time—if you haven't made any sort of land transportation arrangement—start out upstream, against the current if there is one, or against the wind. Then, on the return trip you can drift with the current or run with the wind. Since you will be more tired coming back than going out, you'll like canoeing more if the return trip is easier than the going.

Pole, Paddle & Portage: A Complete Guide to Canoeing. Bill Riviere, Little, Brown & Co., Boston, Toronto, 1974. A former Maine guide, Mr. Riviere has written a clear and good-humored book, useful to beginners and everybody else. It also contains valuable information on canoeing possibilities throughout the United States and Canada and lists guidebooks, local clubs, and other sources of information. Paper.

Basic River Canoeing, Robert E. McNair, American Camping Association, Inc., Bradford Woods, Martinsville, Ind. 46151, 1969. A clear, much used manual. Paper.

You might want to take either of those two books with you on your first forays in a canoe and try to copy the strokes they describe. Either that, or get hold of the *Learn-To-Canoe-Directory* with its listing of 250 places where you can get instruction. It is available free from: Grumman Allied Industries, Inc., Marathon, N.Y. 13803. (They make aluminum canoes.)

Mackens' Guide to U.S. Canoe Trails, James C. Mackens, Le Voyageur Publishing Co., 1319 Wentwood Dr., Irving, Tex. 75061. This lists over a thousand canoeable waters in the United States, both flatwater and whitewater. Paper.

Introduction to Water Trails in America, Robert Colwell, Stackpole Books, Cameron & Kelker Streets, Harrisburg, Pa. 17105, 1977. This one lists rivers scattered throughout the United States, many of them gentle places, ideal for beginners, all within easy reach of 125 urban areas. Paper.

There is a plethora of good books about canoeing, among them many regional guidebooks. A list is available free from Grumman Allied Industries.

There are a few books that, for their mood and spirit, should probably be required reading for anyone thinking about canoeing. Among them:

The Singing Wilderness, Sigurd Olsen, Alfred A. Knopf, New York, 1956. (Or, for that matter, anything and everything by Sigurd Olsen.)

The Survival of the Bark Canoe, John McPhee, Farrar, Straus & Giroux, Inc., New York, 1977. Hardcover.

Canoe, the bimonthly publication of the American Canoe Association, 1999 Shepard Road, St. Paul, Minn. 55116. $6.00 a year.

"Canoe News," a part of the bimonthly *Wilderness Camping,* 1597 Union Street, Schenectady, N.Y. 12309. $5.90 a year.

Associations

By joining a canoe club you have the possibility of learning both fundamentals and whitewater techniques. For information about local clubs, inquire of the following national organizations:

American Canoe Association, 4260 East Evans Avenue, Denver, Colo. 80222. There are thirteen regional divisions of the ACA throughout the country. Annual dues include a subscription to *Canoe.*

United States Canoe Association. Sandy Zellers, Membership Chairman, R.R. 1, Winamac, Ind. 46996. Membership includes a subscription to "Canoe News."

American Whitewater Affiliation, Box 51, Wallingford, Conn. 06492. Yearly dues include the bimonthly *American Whitewater Journal.*

Canadian Canoeing Association, 32 Sedgewick Crest, Islington, Ontario. This group functions similarly to the ACA.

All of these organizations are made up of both individual members and club affiliates.

Many general outdoor clubs, like the Appalachian Mountain Club, the Sierra Club, and the American Youth Hostels, are also involved in canoeing. Local canoe clubs can provide information about canoe rentals in their area. So can outdoor and sport shops, chambers of commerce in canoeing regions, and superintendents of state and national parks, forests, and preserves. A state-by-state directory of where aluminum canoes can be rented is available from Grumman Allied Industries, Inc.

Going for a Walk

When I was a child my father and I simply walked out the door, down the street, and into the woods. We spent many mornings walking there, checking the progress of wildflowers, marveling at a snake slithering away in front of us, sometimes surprising a pheasant that flushed, the iridescent blue and green and purple of his plumage gleaming in the sun. Sometimes we talked. More often we walked in silence, walked *for* the silence. Sometimes we stopped at the top of a hill to rest, to see. My father would take a chocolate bar from his pocket and divide it in half. My share was equal to his.

I hike all the time now. I have the lightest and best possible equipment. Ordinarily I wouldn't dream of taking off without proper boots or without making sure my poncho, matches, flashlight, full canteen, and snakebite kit were in my pack. Have I lost so precious a thing as simplicity? I think there's something wrong.

True, my hikes are longer now. They take me into higher country where the weather changes more rapidly than it did in Corbett's Glen. I am interested in the security of being able to walk long distances over difficult terrain with the most possible case. My equipment is wholly practical for that. But have I, out of habit, cut out from *my* life the possibility of simply walking out the door, down the street, and into the woods?

The walks we made, my father and I—and that I still do make, although most often in the course of some longer trek—are like those that follow: along back roads, dirt roads, forgotten roads; down abandoned railroad rights-of-way; on old canal towpaths; and, of course, most of all, through woods.

Dirt Roads

Dirt roads are lovely spots for a walk. It is relaxed walking since you don't have to watch out for roots or rocks or limbs of trees, as you do on hiking trails. But there is also a special sense of adventure, a sense of being on a journey when walking down a road. Roads lead to places.

Part of the pleasure of any kind of walking for me is the very idea of going somewhere—by foot. So ancient a way to travel suits my imagination. A dirt road in Connecticut becomes the road to Bethlehem, to Rome, to the opening of the American West . . . or, for that matter, to some pretty stream in the Housatonic Valley. Dirt roads are for daydreams. When you have gone as far as you like you can always turn around and come back.

Abandoned Railroads

Walking the rails is a time-honored tradition—made somewhat easier, perhaps, by the lack of rails. Ties and tracks have been removed from many abandoned railroad rights-of-way, and the rights-of-way have been specifically designated for the use of hikers, bicyclists, joggers, backpackers, horseback riders, and cross-country skiers.

The trails are gentle and easy. Railroads were built on level ground, or with long, gentle grades so heavy engines could make it uphill. Access to the trails is also generally easy since the rights-of-way cut across urban regions as well as countryside. The trails themselves provide open space—albeit often long and narrow (usually between fifty and a hundred feet wide) open space—in some otherwise developed areas.

The paths are a link with America's history—souvenirs of that lost age when the railroad steamed its glorious way across the continent connecting civilization with wilderness, opening up the future. What an invitation to adventure was the whistle of the train

speeding through the night fields beyond my house!
How far I traveled as a child lying in bed, listening,
waiting nightly for the whistle. As I come across
bridges and tunnels, often left exactly as they were
over the now trackless path, I strongly feel the journeys
that beckoned in that whistle's call.

The tunnels are havens on a hot summer day as you
make your way through country and town, perhaps
past abandoned stations, overgrown farms, a ghost
town. You might even come upon one of the old
station houses given a new life. Some have been re-
cycled into restaurants, shops, cultural centers, or, like
one in Wisconsin, trail headquarters.

Four abandoned rights-of-way (two in Wisconsin,
one in Illinois, one in Texas) have been designated as
National Recreation Trails and are included within
the National Trails System administered by the Department of the Interior's Bureau of Outdoor Recreation. But there are many others as well. Almost 50,000
miles of right-of-way have been abandoned. And there
will be more. Some of them are bound to be near you.

There's also no reason you can't walk the rails that
have not been abandoned. But keep in mind you might
have to share them with a train.

*Right-of-Way, A Guide to Abandoned Railroads in the
United States,* Waldo J. Nielsen, Maverick Publications, Box 243, Bend, Oreg. 97791, 1977. Written by
a train and trail enthusiast, this is a very thorough
guide.

Canal Towpaths

Old canal towpaths are full of history. Who can look at a canal where water still runs and not see upon it that vital, lusty life of the canals—the big, freight-laden boats carrying entire families; dogs and chickens scampering over decks where small children were tied to keep them from falling overboard while boat-borne entrepreneurs selling food and fabric, medicine, books, whiskey—and everything else necessary for life—plied the canals to serve them. The greater efficiency and speed of the railroads may have usurped most of the canals' work, but not the spirit of those days that still permeates the air around their waters.

The towpaths, built for the mule teams that pulled the boats, were also the province of a man whose profession was called "path walker." His job was to keep the canal flowing by trimming errant vegetation along it, repairing slides started by rain, filling in holes made by burrowing animals, and building up any part of the bank that had been washed away.

Towpaths, of course, are splendid places for path

walkers. Today's kind. And some old towpaths have been reclaimed specifically for hiking. Others—the hundreds of miles along dried-up, abandoned canals once used by miners for hydraulic sluicing—especially in California and Georgia—can be easily walked without being officially reclaimed. But there are still other canals lying beneath decades of undergrowth. Bushwhacking through the woods, for instance, you could come upon an old canal lock. For anyone ready to explore, there are historic canal sites that have remained undiscovered for a hundred years or more.

Like railroads, canals passed through urban areas, a fact which means fairly easy access to them today for people living in cities. Parts of many canals are even hidden beneath cities! (If only we could remove the buildings—perhaps build up an occasional fleet of gondolas . . .)

Of all the canal towpaths, the most gloriously developed is that of the Chesapeake and Ohio—184.5 miles, from Cumberland, Maryland, to Georgetown in Washington, D.C. But, while none of the others come near its length, they all provide scenic, level walks. The miles you walk are your own choice. You don't risk boredom by turning around and going back the way you came—anywhere along the path. Everything is always different from the opposite direction.

The best source of further information is the American Canal Society, a sort of clearinghouse for all canal-centered activity. The Society puts much of its energy into trying to make parks out of old canals and encouraging the study and mapping of canals. It also publishes *The American Canal Guide,* a very informative guide to historic canals in the United States and Canada. While the guide concentrates on historical and physical features, access, and potential for recreational use rather than on walking paths, it is clear cnough so that you can probably figure out which canals can be easily hiked.

The American Canal Guide costs $.50 for Part I (The West Coast) and $1.00 for Part II (The South: North Carolina to Florida). Write: Dr. William E. Trout, III, 1932 Cinco Robles Drive, Duarte, Calif. 91010.

The ACS will also send you lists of canals on the National Register of Historic Placcs and canal societies in the United States and Canada.

Towpath Guide to the Chesapeake & Ohio, available from: Potomac Area Council, American Youth Hostels, 1501 16th St., N.W., Washington, D.C. 20036. The only specific guide to a towpath I know of.

The New York Walk Book, New York–Ncw Jersey Trail Conference, Inc. & The American Geographical Society. Doubleday/Natural History Press, Garden City, N.Y., 1977. Gives some description of New Jersey's Morris Canal and Delaware & Raritan Canal. Paper.

Associations

Membership in the American Canal Society costs $6.00 (or $12.00 for *everybody* in your immediate family) and includes the quarterly publication *American Canals*. For more information, write: William H. Shank, P.E. Secretary, American Canal Society, 809 Rathton Road, York, Pa. 17402.

For information about canals in your area you can also write to the state canal societies listed below:

Allen Co.—Fort Wayne Historical Society, 1424 W. Jefferson St., Fort Wayne, Ind. 46804.

C.A.N.A.L., Inc., 36 Lakeview Dr., Lincoln, R.I. 02865.

Canal Museum, Weighlock Building, Erie Boulevard East, Syracuse, N.Y. 13202.

Canal Society of New Jersey, Macculloch Hall, Box 737, Morristown, N.J. 07960.

Canal Society of New York State, 311 Montgomery Street, Syracuse, N.Y. 13202.

Canal Society of Ohio, 550 Copley Road, Akron, Ohio 44320.

Chesapeake & Ohio Canal Association, 104 Valley Road, Bethesda, Md. 20016.

Cumberland & Oxford Canal Association, 36 Lester Drive, Portland, Me. 04103.

Delaware & Hudson Canal Historical Society, 300 N. Ohioville Road, New Paltz, N.Y. 12561.

Farmington Canal Corridor Association, P.O. Box 24, Plainville, Conn. 06062.

Fort Hunter Canal Society, Fort Hunter, N.Y. 12069.

Georges River Canal Association, Warren, Maine 04864.

Hugh Moore Park, 200 S. Delaware Drive, Easton, Pa. 18042.

Illinois & Michigan Canal Museum, Will County Historical Society, 803 S. State Street, Lockport, Ill. 60441.

Middlesex Canal Association, Box 33, Billerica, Mass. 01821.

Pennsylvania Canal Society, 818 Belmont Avenue, Johnstown, Pa. 15904.

Many of these societies publish newsletters for their members. You might ask them about canals *and* membership.

A Walk in the Woods

A short walk in the woods is a chance just to walk, to look at wildflowers or birds, to forage for food, or simply to find a lovely tree to sit under.

City, county, and state parks all provide places for walks in the woods. Some have paths for which there are maps available at park headquarters or local outdoor stores. Others have paths that can easily be followed without maps as far as you care to follow them. Many have marked nature trails (as do many National Parks) where, in a short walk, various things—trees, flowers, geologic formations, animal habitats—are identified for you either on the spot or in free, printed guides available at the park's headquarters or nature center. Don't worry about remembering names. The real function of these guides is to give you an idea of how much there is around you in a very small space and to help you look at things differently when you go off for a walk on your own.

You can *see* things without their names. Names, after all, are entirely external, although knowing a few helps you feel familiar, intimate—like knowing the name of a person. If really looking at things should make you curious about their names, there are field guides to everything—wildflowers, ferns, rocks, birds, butterflies—that are easy to carry (see end of chapter).

Walks can be made over a short distance. These are walks for people who enjoy the outdoors because it is natural. I have met people for whom hiking seems to be only distantly related to being outdoors, becomes instead a display of physical prowess. That's OK, but in its single-minded assault on the landscape, it lacks both the gentleness and the passion of nature. Nature is made up of grizzly bears and sequoias, but it is made up even more of spiderwebs and star flowers. You have to go slowly and gently to see them.

Peer beneath things. In forests, shy wildflowers like violets or Canada dogwood or trillium—or probably a hundred others—hide beneath and behind this year's green, while some fungi—like wondrous Indian pipe— lie hidden beneath dead leaves piling up forever on the forest floor. Look inside the cracks in rocks to see what tiny, mighty wildflower dares to grow there, its roots reaching far down for a nurturing place, its small petals able to withstand brutal wind and storm.

Look at a whole tree. The color and texture of its bark are as special as the shape and color of its leaves. Watch a tree through a year of seasons—from its first tiny buds to its flowering to the unfolding of its leaves, gaining almost visibly day by day in color and size and richness. Watch the colors change. Each kind of tree has its own colors, its own timing. Some hold insistently on to dried brown leaves throughout the winter, when the winter limbs against the sky define your tree as it can never be defined in other seasons.

Crush the needles of an evergreen between your fingers; scratch the bark to see if it smells the same as the needles; learn the tree from its scent. Look at the needles of various evergreens. How different the pines are from the firs, the spruce. Sit for a while beneath a tree—and wonder about its roots.

If you are at all uneasy about walking anywhere except around the block by yourself or with inexperienced friends or family, you might investigate a hiking club. They exist throughout the country, particularly in urban areas. You can get a list of them either from your city or state chamber of commerce or from outdoor stores specializing in hiking and backpacking equipment. (And some are listed at the end of this chapter.) Many of these clubs sponsor hikes on weekends, some of them geared to new hikers. But keep in mind that even though these will be relatively easy hikes, you will still have to go at the group's pace, which may or may not be your own, and you will be part of a group. Groups do not experience all the things two or three people do. One advantage of getting involved, however, is that you will find out where the trails are in your region, how to get to them, and what the terrain is like.

You might find that short and gentle walks will entice you to longer and more rugged walks. And more equipment. I guess one of the prices of pleasure is sophistication—the loss of simplicity. Never mind. More rugged hiking is pleasure of another sort. Yet I think in the end the adventure is the same.

A Field Guide to Trees & Shrubs (Northeastern & Central North America), George A. Petrides, Houghton Mifflin Co., Boston, 1973.

A Field Guide to Rocky Mountain Wildflowers, John J. Craighead, Frank C. Craighead, Jr., and Ray J. Davis, Houghton Mifflin Co., Boston, 1963.

A Field Guide to Wildflowers of Northeastern & North Central America, Roger Tory Peterson and Margaret McKenny, Houghton Mifflin Co., Boston, 1977.

AMC Field Guide to Mountain Flowers of New England, Stuart K. Harris, Jean H. Langenheim, Frederic L. Steele, and Miriam Underhill, Appalachian Mountain Club, Boston, 1977. The definitive guide to mountain flowers in the region.

New Field Book of American Wild Flowers, Harold W. Rickett, G. P. Putnam's Sons, New York, 1963.

The Tree Identification Book, George W. Symonds, William Morrow, New York, 1973. Good and thorough. It identifies trees through the leaves, bark, flower, fruit, twigs, and buds with clear photos. Paper.

Outdoor stores in every region of the country carry guides to wildflowers and trees in their region. These are always small, light, and easy to carry.

Outdoor Clubs

Adirondack Mountain Club, RD 1, Ridge Road, Glens Falls, N.Y. 12801.

Appalachian Mountain Club, 5 Joy Street, Boston, Mass. 02108.

Green Mountain Club, 108 Merchants Row, Rutland, Vt. 05701.

Iowa Mountaineers, P.O. Box 163, Iowa City, Ia. 52240.

Mazamas, 909 N.W. 19th Avenue, Portland, Oreg. 97209.

The Mountaineers, P.O. Box 122, Seattle, Wash. 98101.

Potomac Appalachian Trail Club, 1718 N Street, N.W., Washington, D.C. 20036.

The Sierra Club, 530 Bush Street, San Francisco, Calif. 94108. Inquire about regional chapters—they exist throughout the country.

American Youth Hostels, Box T, National Campus, Delaplane, Va. 22205. While not the same sort of outdoor club as the others listed, it does sponsor many outdoor activities—and not just for "youth." Inquire about a chapter near you.

The clubs listed are among the largest. Most of them have regional chapters and all are involved in a variety of outdoor activities—hiking, skiing, canoeing, conservation, and so forth.

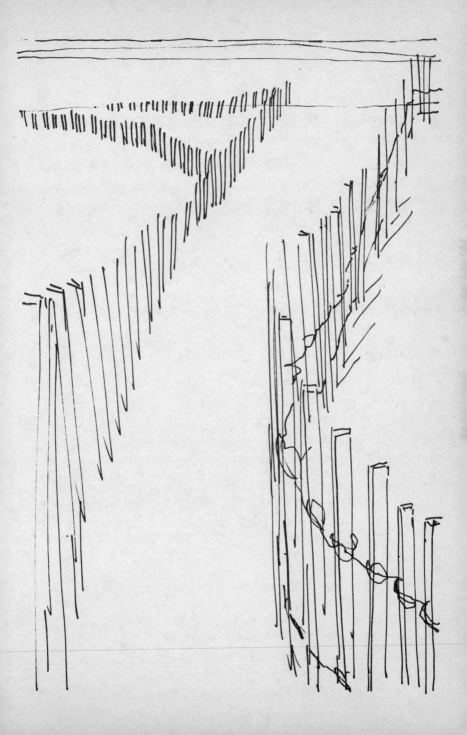

Summer

The sweet, hot smell of summer comes off the dusty back roads. The fields are full of berry bushes heavy with fruit. Paths through the pine woods lead to secret moss-soft places. Rushing streams shimmer over stones they themselves have carved, while silver fish flutter in and out of dark and sunlit places.

The air enfolds, caresses. Who can be blamed for spending hours lying in the shade of a huge old maple? Forgotten pleasure? Well, forgotten by many. Laziness is out of fashion. Doing absolutely nothing but lying in the cool grass and watching the day change has lost out to tennis camps, dirt bikes, and whitewater rafting. But to me the essence of summer is contained in the softness of sky and grass, the slow movement of a hawk, the delicacy of a butterfly lighting on a flower, the sound of gentle water lapping at the shore, all of it enveloping me beneath my maple.

A Short Walk in
Black Rock Forest

The softness of the day makes me lazy and I climb
slowly the short way up to the path junction. A gentle
breeze cools the woods. The thick green of the trees
in full leaf shelters me from the sun and isolates the
hillside from the valley. It is not until I come to the
first viewpoint that I have any sense how high I am
above the valley.

The brook is not very full. It meanders along as
lazily as I do. With a short step over water I climb
on to a boulder where I can sit surrounded by the
brook. The water is clear, hypnotizing, as the sun
jumps and sparkles on it, the sun's motion controlled
by the movement of water and wavering leaves.

The blue marked trail is completely dry and I cannot
even imagine last spring's stream. Everywhere, as far
as I can see, the laurel is in bloom. At waist level the
forest is entirely pink.

Echo Rock is in full sun. The sun feels good, a relief
from the green enclosure of the forest. Below me

Sutherland Pond is so inviting that I begin to consider how far I can dive. I become every Polynesian who ever poised to dive seemingly hundreds of feet into a perfect blue lagoon in glorious Technicolor. The daydream takes over—and I become cool enough without diving. In the distance, between and above the mountains to the south, three hawks soar and swoop.

The path to the pine woods is hot. The high trees are far enough back so that the sun reaches the path, but so does air; I immerse myself in the air and sun and golden heat. Even before I reach the pines their scent comes out to meet me. Stepping inside the woods is like hitting a cold patch of water in a warm lake. I sit down on the soft needles beneath a tree, lean back for a cold drink. It is silent here. There is not even the sound of a bird.

The top of Black Rock greets me with its eternal wind, a great gift on a summer walk. Today I do not cross to the back for shelter but sit on the highest point where wind and sun both have full access to me.

Berrying

I like all berries except thimbleberries. I have so un-
reasonable a prejudice against thimbleberries that I
will not even *taste* thimbleberry jam, which I am told
is delicious. My prejudice stems from hours of making
my way through thimbleberry patches while hiking
on Isle Royale in Lake Superior. They grow there
utterly wantonly. High and thick, by late summer their
maplelike leaves overlap the path, completely oblit-
erating it unless you keep your eyes constantly down
on your feet, where the path *is* discernible. But that
way, of course, you bump into various things, and you
can't keep a proper lookout for moose. (One of the
things I sometimes feel a need for is keeping a proper
lookout for moose.) Besides, the plant is often over
five feet tall, which provides me with a sense of being
submerged in it. To add insult to injury, the fruit, ripe
in August and September, hangs there, looking tan-
talizingly like a raspberry and then tasting . . . well,
tasting like a thimbleberry. I have eaten only one.

My favorite berry—blueberry—grows on my fa-

vorite landscape—high, rocky, open. (Actually, it
grows virtually everywhere, except deserts. Michigan
and New Jersey are the prime producers. By blueberry
I mean all the varieties of blueberries and huckleberries.) There is such a rocky, open area in the
Shawangunks—a low mountain ridge midway between
New York City and the Catskills—where I sometimes live. In the early part of the century the vegetation up there was deliberately burned over to encourage the growth of blueberries by people who made
their living, such as it was, picking blueberries. The
area remains lush with berries even though commercial
berrying has robbed those people of a career.

Weekends find a lot of hikers up there. I usually
go during the week, particularly in blueberry season.
I begin, fully intent on the berries, picking quickly to
fill my basket, already tasting the pie that will evolve
from this trip. But gradually I forget, almost, what
it is I am about, become lost instead in this place. The
ground is blue with berries, the sky is blue. In between
is gray rock, the dark green berry leaves, wind-dwarfed
pines, silence, and time.

Somehow, I never manage to quite fill my basket
before the sun starts down.

Picking berries, even thimbleberries, if you happen
to pass them is fairly instinctive. But what a good
excuse berry picking is for going outside and doing
something on a lovely summer's day. Even people who
live in cities can get on a bus or train that's heading
out of town and probably, within an hour's ride, find
themselves a berry patch. All it takes is the courage
to buy a bus ticket to some totally arbitrary spot. Of
course, if you *know* where the berries are, that's the

spot to aim for. If there is a local botanical society you might check with it. Otherwise, buy a ticket to the smallest nearby town with a bus stop. (You do want to be able to get home again, and while buses will often let you off in the middle of nowhere if you ask the driver, they will usually pick you up only at a proper stop. You should at least know where to find one.) Look around as you enter town. Can you spot some dirt roads from the bus? If not, ask at the bus stop or a nearby gas station; then spend your afternoon ambling along the road you've found. If there are hiking trails in the neighborhood, a short walk along the beginning of one (you can return the same way) might net you a good berry patch.

While you're about your berry picking, you may discover a cool and bubbling brook, a sunny meadow full of flowers, a fragrant pine forest, a charming town. (You may discover any or all of these even if you don't find a berry patch.) And all you need is bus fare, a picnic lunch, and a container for your berries— that is, if you can bear to put them into something besides your mouth.

But you could also add to your picnic lunch by carrying a plastic bowl, a spoon, and a small thermos of cream to pour over blueberries, raspberries, black-berries, strawberries. Or perhaps some red wine to pour over strawberries or raspberries, or for that matter, a bottle of champagne to pour over straw-berries. While you gather berries, leave the champagne to chill in a stream. Make sure the bottle is firmly wedged between some rocks or tied to something on shore so it won't be swept downstream and out to sea, only to be found by a beachcomber years later in

Australia. You might also make sure that the particular stream is not a popular picnic spot (easily accessible streams often are on weekends) or your champagne may never have a chance to float to Australia.

Nothing seems more luxurious to me than fresh berries sprinkled with a little sugar for breakfast on a camping trip. (Or any other time, although if I'm not living out of my pack I'd skip the sugar and use cream.) In the berry months there's no reason to be without them, wherever you live, except possibly in the desert.

Beginning with the first strawberries in mid-June, there are berries enough to get you through the summer and on into fall. (And longer. Since berries—particularly blueberries—freeze well, you can eat at Christmas those you picked in July. See end of chapter.) The common berries, those everyone knows, are safe for everyone to pick. Less common ones require a bit more discernment. There are berries, like other wild plants, which are poisonous. If you cannot positively identify a berry, don't eat it.

But back to wild strawberries. They look like the commercial ones, only smaller. But their sweet taste is unrivaled by commercial berries. Their leaves, by the way, can be used for a tea that is a remedy for colds, in case you go berry picking with a cold. Wash the leaves, boil them for about ten minutes, let them steep a while, drink, and be cured. Or, once you're home, dry, crush and store them for future teas . . . and colds.

July and August (earlier at low altitudes in warm places) bring all the raspberries. I've already mentioned thimbleberries, a member of the family. The other raspberries are different—scrumptious. Wild red raspberries are virtually indistinguishable from domestic raspberries. Except that they're free. Among the most abundant berries in the northern states and Canada, they can be found on open ground, or in forest clearings. Black raspberries are rarer, and tarter, than red. They are also more self-protective with their strong, sharp thorns. (Berry picking should be done adequately clothed to protect yourself from scratches.) Blackberries, on the other hand, are among the most common of wild berries. They are distinguished from black raspberries—in case you care—by their white, pithy core. They grow in waste ground, along roadways and fence lines, in logged-over areas, on mountain rock slides and on sand beaches. They grow in shade or sun, but the berries in sunny places taste better. Salmonberries are less common. These are golden, a little larger and longer than red respberries, but totally recognizable as a raspberry.

Some berries are not so much for eating as for drinking. Elderberries are a good example because they are easy to identify and to pick. Purple-black, these berries grow in clusters on shrubs that can be as high as twelve feet. They like stream banks and woods —any rich, moist soil. The clusters are at the end of a stem which supports a number of leaf stalks with five to eleven leaflets arranged in opposite pairs on the stalk. The oval, serrated leaflets have points at the end. All you have to do is gently pull the berries all off at once, directly into your container. To make your drink (which you can't have until tomorrow), mash the berries and add water; then let the mixture stand overnight. In the morning, strain the mash, add a bit of honey. Very restorative. (Note: DO NOT use red elderberries, which are poisonous.)

Red bilberries, however, are not poisonous. You'll find these low, light-green plants with their thin, shiny leaves and bright pink berries—looking for all the world like blueberries except for their color—at high altitudes. They are also called pink blueberry, pink huckleberry, red alpine blueberry, and grouse whortleberry (I don't know where that last one came from). They can be found on hillsides as high as 7000 feet. Ripe from the end of July through October, they can be eaten like blueberries—baked, for instance, into grouse whortleberry pie. The Indians used them in pemmican. But then, the Indians used virtually every edible berry in pemmican. (Pemmican is a highly concentrated, preserved food made of meat, fruit, nuts.)

I wonder if pemmican improves the taste of thimbleberries?

The Compleat Blueberry Cookbook, Elizabeth W. Barton, Phoenix Publishing, Canaan, N.H. 03741, 1974.

About freezing berries: They should all be washed and dried. Freeze blueberries on a cookie sheet in a single layer. Then divide them as you like and pack them into plastic bags. They retain their plumpness when defrosted, but they are also good simply popped into your mouth frozen, like a tiny popsicle. Other berries should be sugared and frozen in plastic freezer containers. They never retain their original firmness when defrosted, but they are still much better than no berries.

Journey by Horse or Mule

Riding a mule seems to be a forgotten pleasure mainly
for the mule. I rode one up a small mountain in
Greece. That is, I sat on one while it went backwards,
sideways, and noways. After a while I got off and
pulled it up behind me. It took much longer to get to
the top of that mountain than it would if I had not
been pulling a mule. But one can hardly abandon one's
mule.

In Yosemite National Park mules are used to haul
supplies up to the High Sierra camps used by hikers
and riders. Mules also carry people on trips of several
days from one High Sierra camp to the next. (So do
horses.) People I met in the camps (I was traveling
by foot) seemed uniformly delighted with their mules.
One woman proudly announced she'd gotten hers to
leap over a fallen tree. Maybe those Yosemite mules
prefer carrying people to freight, because some of
those I met carrying freight made my Greek mule seem
like the most willing, docile, loving, attentive creature
on earth.

The nice things about mules are that they are wonderful looking, small, strong, sure-footed, and steady —when moving. They are also quite steady when refusing to move. I just like the *idea* of mules. They seem to me so much a part of the American West. They are suited to the steep, rocky terrain of Western mountains. Far easier to ride than horses, they are ideal animals for inexperienced riders who want to get into the backcountry but don't want to hike. Anybody can ride a mule.

Horses, of course, are something else. Nobody's forgotten about horses. I was standing on an Oregon beach one early morning when the mist was broken by a rider on a white horse. The Oregon coast is sand and sea and huge gray rocks jutting out of the sea. The horse galloped at the edge of the water, sand spraying up behind, sea spraying up behind. There seemed to be nothing on earth at that moment but the colors of sand and sea and sky and rock, and a white horse as fast as the wind.

In New York City there is a stable on my street. Early on weekend mornings—and many other mornings as well—local traffic en route to the park consists of horses, bicycles, joggers, and dogs. Just the *street* is a forgotten pleasure. Outside of the city, many people ride horses through the wilderness. Parks often maintain horse trails as well as hiking trails. Many abandoned railroad rights-of-way have been designated as horse trails. Those days when one *had* to spend several days on horseback to get from one place to another are now possible by choice. Stables are to be found near every park where there are horse trails, and you can hire a horse for hours or for days.

But riders are hardly limited to parks and official trails. Dirt roads, old carriage roads, other—unofficial—trails are everywhere. If you live in horse country, riding is taken for granted. If you live in cities or suburbs, it may be a way into the outdoors you hadn't thought much about; yet, like going for a country walk, it is a simple pleasure accessible with a minimum of effort. Outside cities, horses are cheaper than they are within cities, but the city dweller must add the cost of getting to the horse to the cost of hiring the horse. Of course, that cost buys you a day in the country. But a horse in the city buys you a glorious hour before going to the office.

For inexperienced riders, guided horseback trips—an hour or a day long, or even several days or weeks long—can be a good way of learning by doing. This is more expensive and therefore less "simple" than just going off and hiring a horse for an hour or a week, but it still has the proper aura about it—unmechanized pleasure. Pack trips, of days or weeks, are for riders of every level of experience. While experienced wilderness campers can pack themselves into the backcountry, anyone can arrange with an outfitter to *be* packed in. The outfitter will provide horses, camping gear, and trained guides. Or, if you are an experienced horseperson (but inexperienced packer), you might want the outfitter to pack you in, leave, and then reappear on some appointed day to pack you out again. Pack trips can be completely tailored to your wishes.

Other commerical riding possibilities include a stay at a guest ranch, where you can ride all day without having to camp out; a horseback trip over the High Sierra Circuit; a trip more or less from inn to inn in

Vermont or Wyoming, in which you arrive by horse while your luggage is taken by car. But whatever kind of trip you choose, whether it's for an hour or a week, if you have never sat on a horse before, there are a few practical clothing necessities of which you should be aware. Wear shoes or boots with heels which will keep your foot from sliding through the stirrup in case of a fall. (If your foot slides through you could be dangled and dragged.) And wear long pants. Sitting on a horse does not feel like sitting on a bicycle.

Besides, who ever rode off into the sunset in shorts and sneakers?

Horseback Vacation Guide, Steven D. Price, Stephen Greene Press, P.O. Box 1000, Brattleboro, Vt. 05301, 1975. Directory of everything having to do with horses—including information on dude ranches, sleigh rides, and covered-wagon trips.

Horse Packing in Pictures, Francis W. Davis, Charles Scribner's Sons, New York, 1975. A very clear book written by a man who teaches horse packing to 4-H groups and riding schools. Drawings illustrate all the techniques. Hardcover.

Horses, Hitches and Rocky Trails, Joe Back, Swallow Press, Inc., 1139 S. Wabash Avenue, Chicago, Ill. 60605, 1977. Also a good book on horse and mule packing—and also clearly illustrated.

Horse Trails in New York State, New York Department of Environmental Conservation, 50 Wolf Road, Albany, N.Y. 12201. Provides information on trails and route guides and contains maps of Adirondack, Catskill, and other horse trails.

Michigan Riding & Hiking Trails—Northern Lower Peninsula, Michigan Department of Natural Resources, Lansing, Mich. 48926

California Riding and Hiking Trails, State of California, Division of Beaches and Parks, Department of Natural Resources, Sacramento, Calif.

Illinois Prairie Path, Illinois Prairie Path, 616 Delles, Wheaton, Ill. 60187

National Parks of the United States: A Map and Guide shows which national parks maintain horse trails. (It also shows every other facility in every national park.) Write: Superintendent of Documents, U.S. Government Printing Office, Washington, D.C. 20402. Ask for stock number 024-005-00546-3, send $1.00 (their minimum for a mail order), and prepare to wait a long time. They're very slow. Inquire directly of park headquarters (addresses are in the brochure) about the location of stables.

Associations

Many conservation organizations sponsor pack trips. For information contact:

Wilderness Society, 1901 Pennsylvania Avenue, N.W., Washington, D.C. 20006. Ask for the brochure *A Way to the Wilderness,* which lists their trips.

The Sierra Club, 530 Bush Street, San Francisco, Cailf. 94108. They run a few horseback trips, as well as some where *you* hike but a mule or burro carries your gear. The Sierra Club finds burros more affectionate than mules. Trips are open to members or applicants for membership.

American Forestry Association, 1319 Eighteenth Street, N.W., Washington, D.C. 20036. Ask for their brochure, *Trail Riders of the Wilderness.* They run trips in the East as well as the West.

National Wildlife Federation, 1412 Sixteenth Street, N.W., Washington, D.C. 20036. Ask for their brochure about pack tours.

American Youth Hostels, National Campus, Delaplane, Va. 22205. They sponsor an annual trail ride through Pennsylvania Dutch country—the only organization besides the American Forestry Association that runs trips in the East.

Trail Riders of the Canadian Rockies, P.O. Box 6742, Station D, Calgary, Alberta, Canada T2P 2E6. Ask for their schedule of trips through the Canadian Rockies.

Commercial Packers and Dude Ranches

For information about commercial packers and dude ranches inquire of your state chamber of commerce or have a look at the *Horseback Vacation Guide* (see above) or *Adventure Trip Guide,* available for $3.50 from Adventure Trip Guides, Inc., 36 E. 57th Street, New York, N.Y. 10022.

For trips on horse or mule over the High Sierra Circuit, contact: Yosemite Park and Curry Co., Yosemite National Park, Calif. 95389. Phone: (209) 372-4611 or, in California, toll free (800) 692-5811.

For trips from inn to inn in Vermont or Wyoming contact: Green Trails, Dept. A, Brookfield, Vt. 05036, Att: Chris Williams & Ed Taylor. Phone: (802) 276-2012.

L. D. Frome, RFD Afton, Wyo. 83110. Phone: (307) 886-5240.

Guided mule trips for several hours or a couple of days can be made into (and out of) the Grand Canyon. You must be at least twelve years old and weigh under 200 pounds. For more information write: Superintendent, Grand Canyon National Park, Box 129, Grand Canyon, Ariz. 86023

Caving

Last summer, while hiking on a little-used path in the Catskills, I came across a deep cave formed out of bluestone (a blue-gray sandstone whose quarrying was one of the major nineteenth-century industries of the Catskills). The cave was filled with an enormous boulder.

Even while I was thinking "boulder," I knew it was an illogical thought. Boulders don't squeeze into caves. Nor do caves contour themselves tightly around boulders. I looked again. The path and the cave were in shadow so it was difficult to make out the form, but after a while I realized it was an animal, curled up, its head resting on its haunches. A deer, I decided. Again, I knew as I decided, that "deer" was a thought as illogical as "boulder." Deer do not bend down and crawl into caves. A cloud shifted, a ray of sunlight suddenly appeared—and as quickly went. In that instant I saw the bear. I remained staring into the cave, insistent that the sun come back so that I could see the bear again to make sure. If it was a bear, why wasn't it moving? Why didn't it sense me? I was sure but still felt I had to make sure. Then, before more sun could come, it occurred to me: If it was a bear, why wasn't *I* moving? I turned then, walked, rather more quickly than usual, down the path the remaining mile to the road, and left the forest.

Now I believe the bear was dead.

That was caving of a sort.

One brilliantly sunny, hot Kentucky morning, four of us climbed up onto a rock platform, then crawled, one by one, through the entranceway of a cave, and stood up inside the earth. But for the crack of light from the entrance and the beams from our flashlights, we were in utter darkness. By the time all four of us were inside we had light enough from the flashlights to get some idea of the vastness we had felt on entering. The high-ceilinged room receding beyond the shadow of our lights was hung with hollow tubes of minerals which were slowly becoming the same solid rock as the stalactites that had already formed. Stalagmites made their way up from the floor and, where the forms joined, our lights showed us solid columns of white and yellow, gray, black, red. The constant dripping from the ceiling was the only sound in the awesome silence. Surely we had entered some great primeval temple where obeisance to the eternal was marked by falling drops of water. Depositing their minerals, drop by drop, layer upon layer, they made their way into and through subterranean time.

An opening at the far end of the room led us into a smaller room where a broad ledge enclosed a black pool of water. Very cautiously we made our way, often crawling when the ceiling came down too low for us to stand, toward another doorway. Above our heads, and somewhat to the left of where we entered, a sliver of light slipped into this third room. It surprised us. Adjusted now to a world of no light but the circles from our flashlights, we had forgotten the light of day.

We played our lights around the walls. They were fully lined with bats. It seemed to me that in some places there were many layers of bats, but maybe that was an emotional reaction to seeing such an immense covering of them. They simply hung there, a wild tapestry. We remained long enough to assure ourselves that the bats did, indeed, cover all the walls. Then, cautiously staying away from the walls, we made our way to the light. The bats thinned out as we neared the light. At a rock shelf leading to the light and the exit there were no bats. We had to reach high with our arms and stretch long with our legs, but managed to haul ourselves up onto the cold, damp shelf and then squeeze through the opening onto more rock.

The sun seemed blinding now that we had lived so intensely without it. The outside rock was still hot. The heat felt good. We hadn't realized how cold we had become. Like reptiles eager to warm their sluggish blood in the first spring heat, we crawled out on the rocks. We lay a long time on those hot rocks.

That was also caving.

Bears in the Catskills and bats in Kentucky—between the two there is a vast world of caves and cave life. The Kentucky cave, a proper limestone cavern, is probably what most people think of when they think of caves. It's the kind in which Tom Sawyer and Becky Thatcher got lost. But other kinds of caves

—formed by volcanoes and by ice, by waves and streams and tumbling boulders—are just as much caves.

In external caves, or the thresholds of subterranean caves, you may see bats, skunks, raccoons, porcupines, rats, moths, mosquitoes and other insects, snakes, and, of course, bears—all of whom have gone there for protection from predators or from the weather. Other animals—some salamanders, spiders, millipedes, crustaceans, various insects, etc.—live in the dark zone of caves but could, if they chose, live outside. Then there is that special realm of the blind: animals without eyes at all, or with tiny eyes; some of the animals dead white, without any pigmentation. Here are the blind cave fish and white salamanders, insects with extra-long antennae, all those who are born, live, and die in darkness.

Caves have been explored and lived in ever since the first person discovered the first cave. But exploration always requires a certain amount of care, however simple the cave. Each kind of cave presents its own dangers. Common to most caves are the possibilities of flash floods after a heavy rainfall and the presence of a rattlesnake asleep at the entrance.

The world of caves, formed over millions of years, is delicate beyond all others. Even the fragile high mountains are healed by weather and time; the most desecrated forests grow back in time. But inside a cave there is neither rain nor wind to help erase the litter and markings of vandals. It is the one place where time has nothing to do with seasons. It is no wonder that cavers are highly protective of this special world, rarely disclosing cave locations. The best, and easiest, way to learn where they are and how to explore them safely is through a caving club.

You might also experience a cave in any of the commercial caves which exist all over the country. Here are caves of every type, and many avid cavers got their start that way.

Of course, when you are always looking, you are bound to come across your own caves. They are entirely yours to explore—once you've checked them out for bears . . .

American Caves and Caving, William R. Halliday, M.D., Harper & Row, New York, 1974. Well written and informative about all kinds of caves. Hardcover.

The Amateur's Guide to Caves and Caving, David R. McClurg, Stackpole Books, Harrisburg, Pa., 1973. Endorsed by the National Speleological Society.

Speleology, The Study of Caves, George W. Moore and Brother G. Nicholas, National Speleological Society, Cave Avenue, Huntsville, Ala. 35810, 1977. A superb introduction to the science of caves. Paper.

The Life of the Cave, Charles E. Mohn and Thomas L. Poulson, McGraw-Hill Book Co., New York, 1966. Marvelous cave photos. Developed with World Book Encyclopedia and produced with the cooperation of the U.S. Department of the Interior.

Visiting American Caves, Howard N. Sloane and Russell H. Gurnee, Crown Publishers, New York, 1977. A guidebook to all American caves open to the public.

Associations

The National Speleological Society has about 115 chapters, called "grottos," throughout the country. For one near you, write: National Speleological Society, Cave Avenue, Huntsville, Ala. 35810.

Butterflying

The lawn is emerald green, the sky clear, the sun warm. Flower beds, a profusion of color and scent matched in gaiety and pattern only by butterflies, lie at the base of the garden walls. A child dressed in white runs, arms wide open, scattering a bouquet of butterflies, which rise up from the garden like so many flying flowers, flutter randomly about, and land exactly where they started from.

I've had my eye on a red admiral for an hour. I am fascinated by the tiny specks of blue at the end of his hind wings, just there before the edges change from the dark color that covers most of the wings to the brown-dotted red edge. His fore wings have a red and a white stripe and some white dots. He is quite beautiful. (But how I would love to see some of the colors of tropical butterflies—the jewel-like purple-spotted swallowtail of New Guinea's mountain forests; the giant blue swallowtail—an ultimate in art nouveau design—that lives in African forests; or the phenomenal blue morphos of South America whose color is beyond any other perception of blue I have ever had. But I want to see them *flying* where they live, not in a museum case.) Not of course, that I am not content with my red admiral, with any butterfly, in fact, that comes to my garden to flaunt before me all the glory of the insect world. Even the tiny ones, or maybe especially the tiny ones—the delicate, lacy pearl crescent with the monarch's colors rearranged, or the wonderful chartreusy-yellow alfalfa butterfly, or the common little white cabbage butterfly that is always there in the portulacas—are extraordinary. In their tiny beings they carry the same elaborate structure as the big butterflies.

Catching them has become a game. I raise the cone-shaped net I carry, hold the frame vertical, swing the net sideways toward the flower where my red admiral has settled. With the opening toward the butterfly I scoop my beautiful captive into the net. I swing the net back (with a backhand stroke—nothing like playing tennis to get you in condition to collect butterflies), stop, twist the handle quickly so the bottom of the net falls over the frame to lock the bag, making it impossible for my butterfly to leave.

It is, of course, possible to miss. Butterflies, with their well-developed sense organs, see movement quickly. You raise your arm; the butterfly leaves. The scooped-up butterfly might also simply get out of your net before you are ready to let it go. Stay where you are. It will probably come back to the same spot, and you get a second chance. Always swing gently to keep from injuring the butterfly by rough contact with the bag.

There are times when a chase may be the only way

to make your capture, but usually careful stalking will be more successful. Watch carefully which flowers—or other things—seem to appeal most to which butterflies. They eat nectar and tree sap, rotten fruit, and other decaying matter of varying degrees of acceptability. You need only be present at dinner. Gardens offer the possibility of good collecting—and certainly easy seeing—but they never attract the variety of butterflies you'll find around wildflowers. The best places to start your hunting are among those to go for easy walks—along country roads or railroads, places that give you a good cross-section of all the environments of the specific countryside. Each environment may offer different species of butterflies. If one spot doesn't present much, move on.

Unless you are specifically interested in adding to a collection, there is no reason not to let a captured butterfly go. It seems a great pity to take more butterflies than one needs for a collection and, while it is not so serious with common butterflies, rarer ones—like everything else that is rare—are in danger from being overcollected. The best way to add to a collection, particularly if you live in an area containing relatively few of the more than 50,000 species of butterflies, is from a reputable dealer. *He* gets most of his from butterfly farms.

The joy in catching butterflies is the joy of capturing—for an instant—utter beauty. The satisfaction of being able to let it go is immense.

A Field Guide to the Butterflies of North America, East of the Great Plains, Alexander B. Klots, Houghton Mifflin Co., Boston, 1977. This is really a good, basic nature text, going beyond merely identifying butterflies. It discusses life zones, environments and habitats, and plants in relation to butterflies, as well as how to capture butterflies and what equipment you need. Hardcover and paper.

The World of Butterflies, Michael Dickens and Eric Storey, The Macmillan Co., New York, 1973. Hardcover.

The Year of the Butterfly, George Ordish, Charles Scribner's Sons, New York, 1975. A look into the life of the monarch. Hardcover.

Butterfly nets can be purchased at museums of natural history for about $8 to $10, or you can make your own. There are instructions for making them in *The New Field Book of Nature Activities and Hobbies* (see "Exploring a Creek Bed").

Exploring a Creek Bed

The forest path follows the course of a stony creek. When I take that trail on a summer day I usually eat my lunch on one of the rocks that juts up out of the water. I can put both my lemonade and my feet into the creek to cool. On really hot days I put the rest of me in as well.

I made my way lazily up the path, thinking about the blueberry patch a bit higher up. Suddenly a snake darted out at me from the trunk of a tree, or rather, half a snake uncoiled itself and darted. The back half remained firmly coiled. I hadn't noticed the snake. I hadn't even noticed the tree. In that instant when I instinctively jumped back I had no idea what it was that suddenly swung out at me. It was only after the movements—both the snake's and mine—had been completed that "snake coiled around tree" registered. But from my new position I could not pick out the tree, and the snake had now become absorbed by the tree, or the forest.

I am not afraid of snakes. I like them. But I did

want to know what kind it was before I continued. Although I hadn't seen it clearly, for all my fearlessness, there was no question in my mind but that it was either a cobra or a boa constrictor. Nothing else was possible. This, after all, was the Shawangunks! I allowed myself a full forty-five seconds to catch sight of it, then turned to my left, pushed through a little brush, and came to the edge of the stream. The water flowed through the center of the stream bed, over flat rocks, around higher ones, seeming to settle for moments in deeper little pools, rushing through narrow spaces where rock steps created miniature falls. What more perfect day, I said to myself, to explore this creek bed! Not, of course, that I had ever considered exploring it before. To me streams had always been marvels of cooling beauty, providers of fish and transporation, but *paths* were for walking. But then, I had never before encountered a path lined with boa constrictors.

I took off my boots and tied them to my rucksack, shoved my socks inside, rolled up my jeans and started up the creek bed. The water, which was not very deep, was generally cool, although I felt a not unpleasant rush of warmth when I entered some spots that had been warmed by the sun all morning. I stepped in occasional soft places between rocks where mud oozed up beneath my toes, and on moss-covered rocks whose softness my toes could clutch. (Having slipped on moss-covered rocks in dry creek beds in the past I approached these cautiously, but they felt wonderful.)

Walking in the creek was harder work than walking on the path. Walking through water is not only physically harder than not walking through water, but mentally too, since it takes more concentration. Every step has to be watched. I was so concentrated that I became superaware of everything I could see—little fish darting past me and away, very round and very skinny insects, a few tadpoles in one of the quieter pools, two brilliant blue damsel flies hovering. The pools themselves were fascinating. I had never really noticed how perfectly the rock was hollowed out around the edges of some of them, the bottom of the rock forming a smooth bowl which looked a perfect size to hold one person, sitting.

I continued upstream until I came to an abrupt rise and a waterfall down one side of the rise. The rocks were glistening, wet, and dark but formed broad steps to the side of the falls. It seemed not very difficult to climb to the top. Waterfalls over the steep rock ledges of the Shawangunks are common. Many of them have prodigious amounts of water falling over great heights in spring, but wind down to a trickle by summer. This was a small one.

There was a waterfall not far from my house when I was a child. Summer days were spent sliding down and climbing up and sliding down and climbing up and sliding down one last time a hundred times. I remember it as fun. A little hard on the bottom, possibly, but we were tough. Would it still be fun? I began the climb up, carefully. (I couldn't remember being so careful with that other waterfall. Well, you're alone, I said to myself. Best to be careful alone. Nothing to do with not being a child . . .) The ledge steps were broad enough so that, even though they were slippery, I felt secure as soon as I began to climb. At the top, no more than ten feet up, I crossed over on dry rock to the falls. The water tumbled down rock that also progressed in steps, although worn smooth in places. In any case, it progressed in the right direction—that is, there were no overhangs. The falls simply followed a proper way down, staying close to the rock. I sat down at the edge, pushed (slightly), and slid (or perhaps bounced) and almost at once found myself deposited in the pool of water at the bottom of the falls—which I had already checked out as a proper landing spot. Not bad, I thought. I climbed out of the pool and back to the top of the falls. Even better the second time. I lingered now in the pool, then climbed out to the sun-drenched rock where I had left my pack, leaned back against another rock, and ate.

I never once thought about boa constrictors.

Exploring a streambed can be done on a purely sensual level. How it all feels—moss, wet rock, soft mud under your feet; cold, fast mountain water or the touch of a sun-warmed gentle brook; water wrapping itself around your ankles or knees, swirling in little eddies, sparkling in small pools, rushing away white and foaming over rapids, or calmly meandering over glistening pebbles. But you might also find yourself—for no other reason than the rather intimate association you have with a stream once you are standing in it—curious about the life that is going on around you. For either, or both, these experiences you needn't go far from home. Any stream or part of a stream you come upon will do. If you happen to be driving past a stream, stop your car, or get off the bus, or off your bicycle. Take off your shoes and walk a few feet up the stream. Reach down and look underneath things. Lots of the life of streams (and other fresh water) prefers to hide beneath things. Sponges, for instance. Freshwater sponges may not look much like that nice one in your bath, but those small, jellylike masses wrapped around sticks or stones are, indeed, sponges. You'll often find snails, or salamanders. Streams with muddy bottoms may yield—sometimes with a little digging—mussels and clams. In shady streams, or on cloudy days, you might see crayfish, little lobsterlike animals. (These are eaten in some places, although many streams where crayfish live are so polluted that they are inedible.) In spawning season check out shallow depressions in sand or gravel beds to see if a fish has deposited her eggs there. You might even get to *see* fish laying their great masses of eggs.

MAKE A WATERSCOPE

If you get really involved in looking at things, you might want to make yourself a waterscope so that light reflected from the surface will not interfere with your observations of life below the surface. A waterscope is easy to make with two feet of four-inch-diameter stovepipe. Paint the inside black and cut (or have cut at the hardware store where you get your stovepipe) a window of $\frac{1}{16}$-inch Plexiglas to attach to one end. Use waterproof adhesive tape to attach the window, to seal the pipe seam, and to put over the upper end of the pipe where it touches your face. Bend the pipe to fit your face. Then just stand in the water, or kneel at its edge, push the Plexiglas end under the surface, and wait till something swims up.

A more adventuresome way to have a clear look

underwater—although it requires, perhaps, a river rather than a stream for your looking—is snorkling. All you need is a snorkle—a hollow, curved, plastic tube with a hard rubber mouthpiece—and a diving mask that fits close around your eyes and nose so you can see clearly. (Cost will run from $8 to $36. Swim fins are not necessary.) Most people think of snorkling as something to do over coral reefs in tropical waters full of multicolored fish and other extravaganzas. Outside of the tropics, colors are muted and life less blatantly spectacular, but exploring a river in Wisconsin, for instance, is still adventure. You can cruise over clams, snails, minnows, perhaps an occasional lovely trout. For just a bit more effort than you would use in salt water, you get a chance to experience the river like a fish.

The New Field Book of Freshwater Life, Elsie B. Klots, G. P. Putnam's Sons, New York, 1966. Hardcover.

The New Field Book of Nature Activities and Hobbies, William Hillcourt, G. P. Putnam's Sons, New York, 1970. A good introduction to exploring creeks, ponds, and most of the rest of the natural world. Hardcover.

Rafting

*I knowed the river had begun to rise . . . The June rise used
to be always luck for me; because as soon as that rise begins
here comes cordwood floating down, and pieces of log rafts—
sometimes a dozen logs together; so all you have to do is
catch them . . .*

*One night we catched a little section of a lumber-raft—nice
pine planks. It was 12 foot wide and about 15 or 16 foot long,
and the top stood above water six or seven inches—a solid,
level floor.*

—Huckleberry Finn

For Huckleberry Finn rafting was part of life. Life
was dependent on adventure. It's the same spirit of adventure that has led to today's highly sophisticated running down any available wild river in rubber rafts. The
switch to rubber rafts is eminently practical since, these
days, rivers are relatively bare of log rafts floating
down in the June rise, yours for the catching. And
cutting down trees is out of the question.

Nevertheless, while it may lack a bit in spontaneity,

nothing says you can't buy some logs from a sawmill and build yourself a raft that would do old Huck Finn proud.

The hardest part of this project may be to find a sawmill where you can buy uncut softwood—pine, for instance. Once you do, check whether or not they sell trimmed logs. Untrimmed, the logs' natural knots will keep them from fitting close enough together. Buy seven logs. The longest (and you only need one this length) can be from 12 to 16 feet long at the most and no more than a foot in diameter. The shorter the logs, the narrower they should be. Although there is no reason you can't build a raft with a flat front, what you are aiming for, according to this plan, is a craft with a boat-shaped bow and a rectangular stern. Carve one end of the longest log into a point. Lay out the other logs so that the longest two remaining flank the center one, the next two flank those two, and the two shortest are on the outside. Now slice the ends of these logs on the diagonal, continuing the line of the central point so that you end up with a proper boat shape in front. If the logs are not equally matched you can saw them even at the back of the raft. You now need three pieces of board—1 inch thick by 6 or 8 inches wide, like a shelf—whose length is equal to the width of the raft. These are the cross-strips which will stretch across the raft, on the top side, to hold the raft together. You could nail the boards across, but wooden pegs, or dowels (available in a variety of sizes at lumber yards —make sure they are hardwood because softwood will split) are more authentic and probably stronger. The first cross-strip should be placed toward the front at the place where it can lie across all seven logs before the bow begins to taper. The second should be placed in the middle, and the third a little way in from the back. As for the wooden pegs, drill holes into the cross-strips and logs, lining them up carefully; then simply pound the wooden pegs through. Pegs hold more firmly than nails because they swell once they are in water. Or, for still more durability, you might tie the logs together, across the front, middle, and back. Wrap the rope around the first log, tie a knot and carry the rope over and around the second log, tie a knot, carry the rope over and around the third log, and so on, until all are tied tight—and knotted—together.

Now, if you would like a cabin, get some thick, strong wire or fiberglass or aluminum tubing of the sort used for tent poles—or get ready-made poles from a backpacking store (see end of chapter)—that can be bent into arches or angled so the ends can be secured to the raft floor while the top is high enough to crawl under. Drill small holes part-way into the logs on the back half of the raft, staying in front of the last cross-strip. The holes should be equidistant from the edges of the raft. Place the ends of the wire or tent poles in the holes and stretch a canvas or rip-stop nylon (extra strong, lightweight, uncoated, breathable nylon) over them. Your cabin could end up looking like the top of a covered wagon or a teepee or any of a variety of backpacking tents.

If you put up a sturdy pole at the front of the raft, just behind the first cross-strip, you have a lovely flagpole, or a mast to rig a sail on. It will also help to balance the extra weight of your shelter—with you in it—at the back.

You can control the raft with an oar that serves as

both sweep and rudder at the back of the raft. Find yourself a stout stick for an oarlock—one high enough to allow you to stand while steering. Then drill a hole to set the oarlock in at the middle of the very back of the raft. Whittle the top of the oarlock to a point. To one end of a long pole (like a broom handle), attach a flat board for the blade. Shape the other end to a thinner size to serve as a grip. (Make this very smooth to protect yourself from blisters.) Next, drill a hole through the pole about three feet from the handle's grip, so you can slip the hole over the pointed top of the oarlock. For more control you can also make rudimentary oars on both sides of the raft in exactly the same way as you made the sweep. These should be placed in holes drilled about halfway between the first two cross-strips.

A flat stone toward the bow makes a fireplace suitable either for wood or a camping stove. If you pound some sort of caulking material—cotton, board, vines, anything—between the logs in the cabin and cover that with marine or bathroom caulking and then put down a heavy ground cloth and a couple of air mattresses (Huck would have used straw), you will have a comfortable place to live.

You are now ready to head down the Mississippi. Good luck.

The Adventures of Huckleberry Finn, Mark Twain.

Equipment Sources

Note: Building a raft like this is not inexpensive, although the price of lumber varies from place to place. And many variations are possible. Huck's raft, after all, was "nice pine planks."

For ready-made tent poles and tarps, investigate: Recreational Equipment, Inc., 1525 11th Avenue, Seattle, Wash. 98122; and Eastern Mountain Sports, 1041 Commonwealth Avenue, Boston, Mass. 02215. You can request catalogs from both places. At REI you can purchase a tarp with grommets around the edge. Made of rip-stop nylon, 11 feet by 13½ feet, it costs about $30. EMS has a polyethylene tarp (less strong than rip-stop nylon) with no grommets, 12 feet by 22 feet, for about $15. Tent poles range from $2 to $18, approximately.

Inner Tubes

Sitting in an inner tube on a calm lake is an immensely cool way to read the morning paper on a hot day. On rivers you have the added pleasure of travel. Any river current will carry you along, and what could be more companionable than floating downriver with a friend, engaged in conversation from inner tube to inner tube? Or, take the world for yourself. You have only to lean your head back to become conscious of nothing but moving—lightly, quickly—under the sky. Play with the current. Swivel your tube around to face backward and let it move you around again. Bounce gently through a small rapids. You might even seek out the less gentle rapids, where this diversion takes on the aspect of sport.

Inner tubes can be found, purchased from a tire dealer or gas station for a little over $5, or rented at recreation areas that specialize in such things.

These recreation areas can be quite elaborate, like one in Wisconsin where a chairlift carries floaters, with inner tubes slung over their shoulders, up river.

At the top of a rapids they disembark to ride the rapids down. Visitors also have the possibility of a ten-minute bus ride up river, which provides them with a three-hour float trip back down. The brochure announces this as "The Ultimate in Floating Down the Apple River."

Nothing says you can't find your own ultimate.

Inner tubes can be used as the basis for a raft. A group of cavers have developed one known as the Devil's Icebox raft—named for the cave in Missouri where it evolved. It is made by lashing together half a dozen small inner tubes beneath a simple, flat deck. You can use it even if you are not in a cave.

Tubing, Whit Perry, Great Lakes Living Press, 21750 Main Street, Matteson, Ill. 60443, 1977. An adventure guide to tubing on rivers and snow, including where-to as well as techniques and equipment.

Whitewater Rafting

The ne plus ultra of rafting, of course, is whitewater rafting. Which gets us back to rubber rafts. After World War II, seven-man and ten-man army surplus assault rafts found a new life when a few people began trying them out on whitewater rivers. Very stable and extremely maneuverable, they caught on quickly with professional river guides and the thousands of people each year who take rafting vacations. Now the army surplus rafts have been replaced by rafts specially built for river rafting.

This kind of rafting doesn't qualify as a forgotten or in any way old-fashioned kind of pleasure—except that adventure is old fashioned. It is a natural for people who live on or near white water and a not illogical outcome of simpler river trips. (Still, one of the sights more and more encountered by people in rubber rafts, particularly in the calmer stretches of rivers, is that of someone drifting by in an inner tube. Imagine how *that* feels . . .)

Whitewater rafting requires skill, if you mean to

man your own raft. You don't, after all, simply idly drift down a roaring, raging, broiling, roiling, white-foamed, rock-strewn river. But for anyone with the urge to try it, there are whitewater schools in both East and West. For those just interested in the thrill of being a passenger, commercial raft trips, best known in the canyon rivers of the West, also exist in the East.

Running these rivers is an immediate, insistent link with both nature and the history of America. Their very names conjure up adventure—the Colorado, Rio Grande, Salmon, the Rogue, the Snake, Green, Klamath, Stanislaus, Tuolumne, the Youghiogheny, the Cheat, Chattooga, Flambeau, Wolf, the St. John —names that run like rapids over the tongue.

Whitewater Rafting, William McGinnis, Quadrangle, New York, 1975. *The* book on rafting. Everything you need to know about rubber rafts—equipment and technique—plus a guide to twenty-six good white-water rafting rivers in the United States and useful lists of raft manufacturers, commercial outfitters, and whitewater schools.

Guide to Inflatables (Boat World Guide Series, Number 6), British Book Center, New York, 1975.

Drifting, Steven Jones, Macmillan, New York, 1971.

Commercial Outfitters

Check *Whitewater Rafting* or the *Adventure Trip Guide* (see "A Journey by Horse or Mule") or *Explorer's Ltd. Source Book,* edited by Alwyn T. Perrin, Harper & Row, New York, 1973. Oversized paperback.

Freshwater Fishing

Fishing can come as close to doing nothing as anything I can think of. Not fancy fly fishing. Just the kind where you sit on the river bank, bait a hook on a line, and wait. And dream.

Maybe a mud turtle will turn up or a deer come down to the water. Maybe a butterfly will flutter by, or the hot essence of the day be caught in the brilliance of a dragonfly. Maybe the perch will bite, or a sunfish. Maybe.

Fish are smart. (That is, most fish are smart. I recently read an article in *The New York Times* that said that some trout are quite stupid. But you won't catch trout, stupid or not, fishing with a hook, a line, a pole, and a dream, anyway.) A certain regard for the fish's intelligence and habits may get you a few more fish. They have keen senses of vision, sound, and smell. You can keep both yourself and your shadow out of the fish's line of vision by staying on the shady sides of logs and rocks, the windless side of cliffs or ledges,

and the downcurrent sides of boulders. In order not
to offend their sense of smell (things like gasoline,
tobacco, and onions do), have clean hands, lures, and
bait. Since they also eat on a regular schedule, *when*
you do your dreaming may determine whether or not
you come home with any fish. Early morning, which
gives you a sunrise as well as the possibility of good
fishing, and evening, from sunset on for about an hour,
are the times they are most apt to be interested in
your bait.

Best fishing of all is on a warm, cloudy, humid day,
the kind of day you don't want to do much else anyway. If it happens to follow a bright, moonlit night
with winds from the west, southwest, or south, so much
the better.

It's nice, when fishing, to catch a fish. But it doesn't
really matter if you don't. What you always catch is
a quiet time sitting at the water's edge, or in a gently
rocking boat, a silent time of water and sky and the
movement of natural things.

An ideal way for someone *really* lazy to fish—i.e.
if you'd like to nap while you fish— is to use a bell
pole. Hang an old bell at the end of the pole where
the line is fastened. Put the opposite end of the pole
upright into the river bank. Bait the hook and cast
the line as far out as you can. (In moving water cast
upstream and let the bait drift down.) This is the
most active thing you will have to do. Now lie down
and relax. When a fish gets hooked and struggles, the
bell rings. If you're really lucky, one won't bite all
day.

For the less lazy, this is a good method for gathering a complete dinner. You can fish and forage at the same time, just so long as you stay within earshot of the bell.

Eager for something a bit more active? An old Southern system, jugging for catfish (although it could be other fish as well), provides at least as much exercise for you as it does for the fish. You need a number of empty jugs (half-gallon or gallon wine jugs do fine), tightly corked. Gather an equal number of stout lines, each about five feet long, with a sinker and large hook at the end. Tie one line to the handle of each jug and attach the bait (worms, or cheese tied in cheese cloth to keep it from washing away). Put everything into a boat, row out into the river, and drop the jugs a few feet apart in a line across the middle of the river.

Now comes the action. The jugs will be carried downstream with the current so you have to be ready to follow. As soon as a jug begins to bob and turn, generally moving in every direction at once, you can be reasonably sure there's a fish on the hook. You will now have to chase the fish—that is, catch the jug. This can require vigorous rowing and stamina, since you will soon discover that catching up to the jug doesn't mean *catching* it. As you reach out to grab the jug it will be pulled away by the fish. You just keep moving. If all, or anyway several, jugs catch fish at the same moment, you have a chase worthy of William Friedkin on your hands. Catching the jugs isn't the end, since you must then haul in the line carefully and steadily or the fish will be able to tear himself away from the hook. If you actually capture the fish, be careful. Catfish have long, sharp spines on their dorsal and pectoral fins that can hurt.

There are two vital points to this system. Don't leave any jugs in the river under any circumstances. Don't use this method when you're very hungry.

Where you fish, of course, will determine the kind of fish you'll get. If the pleasure is in the act of fishing, it doesn't much matter. I have passed streams filled with fishermen, wading thigh deep, fishing as if it were their life's work, but doing it with barbless hooks and releasing, as required by law, every fish they catch. But if the catch is the pleasure, then pick your lake or stream accordingly. You will usually get bigger fish out of a lake than a stream. Ask at the local tackle shop what's biting where.

Catch-and-release fishing, by the way, is not uncommon in the national parks, and occurs in some other places as well. There will be signs to that effect. It is always in magnificent streams.

Fishing license requirements differ from state to state and depend on what fish you're after, or what waters within a state you are fishing. Check with your state department of fish and game (see end of chapter).

As for equipment, you can be as elaborate as you like. Or, you can get yourself a bamboo pole and attach some line, a hook, and a sinker ... equipment suitable for dreaming. That is, after all, how this chapter started.

Fishing Made Easy, Arthur L. Cone, Jr., Macmillan, New York, 1976. Paperback.

Basic Fishing, Harlan Major, Funk & Wagnall's, New York, 1968. Paperback.

Fisherman's Handbook, John Power and Jeremy Brown, Charles Scribner's Sons, 1972.

License Information

For current regulations and license requirements, as well as other useful information, contact your state department of fish and game.

Alabama—Dept. of Conservation & Natural Resources, 64 N. Union St., Montgomery, 36130.

Alaska—Dept. of Fish & Game, Subport Bldg., Juneau, 99801.

Arizona—Game & Fish Dept., 2222 W. Greenway Rd., P.O. Box 9099, Phoenix, 85068.

Arkansas—Game & Fish Com., Game & Fish Bldg., 2 State Capitol Mall, Little Rock, 72201.

California—Dept. of Fish & Game, The Resources Agency, 1416 Ninth St., Sacramento, 95814.

Colorado—Dept. of Natural Resources, Div. of Wildlife, 6060 Broadway, Denver, 80216.

Connecticut—Dept. of Environmental Protection, State Office Bldg., Hartford, 06115.

Delaware—Div. of Fish & Wildlife, Dept. of Natural Resources & Environ. Control, Tatnall Bldg., Dover, 19901.

District of Columbia—Metropolitan Police, 300 Indiana Ave., N.W., Washington, 20001.

Florida—Game & Fresh-Water Fish Com., Dept. of Natural Resources, 620 S. Meridian, Tallahassee, 32304.

Georgia—State Game & Fish Div., Trinity-Washington Bldg., 270 Washington St., SW., Atlanta, 30334.

Hawaii—Div. of Fish & Game, Dept. of Land & Natural Resources, 1151 Punchbowl St., Honolulu, 96813.

Idaho—Fish & Game Dept., 600 S. Walnut, Box 25, Boise, 83707.

Illinois—Dept. of Conservation, 605 State Office Bldg., Springfield, 62706.

Indiana—Div. of Fish & Wildlife, Dept. of Natural Resources, 608 State Office Bldg., 300 Fourth St., Des Moines, 50319.

Kansas—Forestry, Fish & Game Com., Box 1028, Pratt, 67124.

Kentucky—Dept. of Fish & Wildlife Resources, Capital Plaza, Frankfort, 40601.

Louisiana—Wildlife & Fisheries Com., 126 Wildlife & Fisheries Bldg., 400 Royal St., New Orleans, 70130.

Maine—Dept. of Inland Fisheries & Wildlife, 284 State St., Augusta, 04333.

Maryland—Dept. of Natural Resources, Tawes State Office Bldg., Annapolis, 21401.

Massachusetts—Dept. of Environmental Resources, Div. of Fisheries & Wildlife, 100 Cambridge St., Boston, 02202.

Michigan—Dept. of Natural Resources, Mason Bldg., Lansing, 48926.

Minnesota—Div. of Game & Fish, Dept. of Natural Resources, 301 Centennial Bldg., 658 Cedar St., St. Paul, 55101.

Mississippi—Game & Fish Com., Robert E. Lee Office Bldg., 239 N. Lamar St., Box 451, Jackson, 39205.

Missouri—Fisheries Div., Dept. of Conservation, 2901 N. Ten Mile Dr., Jefferson City, 65101.

Montana—Fish & Game Dept., Helena, 59601.

Nebraska—Game & Parks Com., P.O. Box 30370, 2200 N. 33rd, Lincoln, 68503.

Nevada—Dept. of Fish & Game, Box 10678, Reno, 89510.

New Hampshire—Fish & Game Dept., Box 2003, 34 Bridge St., Concord, 03301.

New Jersey—Dept. of Environmental Protection, Div. of Fish, Game & Shellfisheries, Box 1390, Trenton, 08625.

New Mexico—Dept. of Game & Fish, State Capitol, Santa Fe, 87501.

New York—Fish & Wildlife Div., Department of Environmental Conservation, 50 Wolf Rd., Albany, 12201.

North Carolina—Wildlife Resources Com., Albemarle Bldg., 325 N. Salisbury St., Raleigh, 27611.

North Dakota—State Game & Fish Dept., 2121 Lovett Ave., Bismarck, 58501.

Ohio—Dept. of Natural Resources, Div. of Wildlife, Fountain Square, Columbus, 43224.

Oklahoma—Fisheries Div., Dept. of Wildlife Conservation, 1801 N. Lincoln, P.O. Box 53465, Oklahoma City, 73105.

Oregon—Dept. of Fish & Wildlife, Box 3503, Portland, 97208.

Pennsylvania—Fish Com., P.O. Box 1673, Harrisburg, 17120.

Rhode Island—Div. of Fish & Wildlife, Dept. of Natural Resources, 83 Park St., Providence, 02903.

South Carolina—Wildlife & Marine Resources Dept., 1015 Main St., Box 167, Dutch Plaza, Bldg. D., Columbia, 29202.

South Dakota—Dept. of Game, Fish & Parks, State Office Bldg. No. 1, Pierre, 57501.

Tennessee—Game & Fish Com., Wildlife Resources Agency, Box 40747, Ellington Agricultural Center, Nashville, 37204.

Texas—Parks & Wildlife Dept., John H. Reagan Bldg., Austin, 78701.

Utah—State Dept. of Natural Resources, Div. of Wildlife Resources, 1596 N.W. Temple, Salt Lake City, 84116.

Vermont—Agency of Environmental Conservation, Fish & Game Dept., 151 Main St., Montpelier, 05602.

Virginia—Com. of Game & Inland Fisheries, 4010 W. Broad St., Box 11104, Richmond, 23230.

Washington—Dept. of Fisheries, 115 General Admin. Bldg., Olympia, 98504.

West Virginia—Dept. of Natural Resources, 1800 Washington St., East, Charleston, 25305.

Wisconsin—Dept. of Natural Resources, Box 450, Madison, 53701.

Wyoming—Game & Fish Dept., Box 1589, Cheyenne, 82002.

For a brochure showing the fishing possibilities in National Parks, including the urban national parks, write: Public Inquiries, National Park Service, U.S. Department of the Interior, Washington, D.C. 20240. The brochure shows which freshwater species exist in each place and where saltwater fishing is possible, and indicates special fishing programs, including catch-and-release, fishing-for-fun, children only, and so forth. Most angling seasons follow state regulations.

Surf Fishing

Quite another experience. While freshwater fishing can be gently engaged in as you doze on a river bank, surf fishing opens you to all the wildness of the sea: the lure of tides, the cry of gulls, and the force of waves; the immensity of a sunrise or sunset; the primeval nature of the beach.

It can also provide you with a super breakfast, not to mention a fascinating way to start your day. Which fish will provide that breakfast depends on where you are and how warm the water is. Some fish migrate, appearing along different parts of different coasts at different times of year. Some come into shallow waters (near beaches) to spawn when the water gets warm enough, then leave again immediately. Not all fish have the same requirements of warmth, so they don't all spawn at the same time in a particular area.

Whatever fish you catch, the ocean will help you land it. It is the nature of surf to throw onto shore anything that gets near the shore . . . which means that surf fishing doesn't require great strength, although you should cast out as far as possible.

The best times for surf fishing are before 10:00 a.m., after 5.30 or 6:00 p.m., and at night, especially during incoming and outgoing tides—whenever water is moving most. (Tide tables are printed in local papers or are available at tackle shops. Tides run about fifty minutes later each day.)

For all the wildness of the sea, there *are* lazy days on the beach—those days when the fishing is slow. There is even a special invention—a sand spike—to encourage a little proper basking in the early sun. A sand spike is a hollow tube that you set upright into the sand and into which you can insert the rod. You then lie back and relax, do a little shelling, watch a few birds, build a sand castle. When a fish bites, your rod will beckon.

In the past few days, when the striped bass have been running off Barnegat Light, I've seen people standing waist deep in the water at high tide. Each time a breaker rolls in, they spring up as far as they can. The wave breaks across their chests. Ordinarily, the fishermen who wade out to the sand bar or stand on the slippery rocks of the jetty—anyplace they will get wet—wear chest-high waders. But these people are all dressed as if they had never expected to leave the dry sand. I haven't seen anyone catch anything yet, but they all seem to be having a wonderful time. I have been told that if one *is* wearing waders, it's a good idea to glue big chunks of felt underneath them to help prevent slipping. But if you are knocked over by breaking surf anyway and your waders get filled with water, you are quite literally sunk, unless you quickly rip off the suspenders and let the waders drop.

Surf fishing does not require a license. No license is ever required for *fishing* tidal waters—which includes as far up rivers and streams as the tide reaches. In some places—various state parks where fishing may be allowed at some distant point accessible only by foot or by four-wheel vehicle—you might need a permit, usually free. (This hasn't much to do with the fish, but with the environment. It is a way of keeping track of how much use a particular spot is getting.)

If you have a long trip home with your fish, stop at the nearest possible place for some dry ice to pack it in, or take dry ice with you in the first place.

As for gear, you can rent all but a few dollars' worth for about $7 to $8 a day from most tackle shops. You will find tackle shops in every town—and along most roads—near fishing. What you need is a surfing rod and reel (the parts you can rent), 20-pound test line (usually), a terminal rig (that's the part that enters the water), and bait. The terminal rig is a three-way swivel. The hook ties onto one side, the sinker on another, and the line on the third. The type of bait, hook, and sinker you need depends on the kind of fish you mean to catch, which depends on the kind of fish running. If you are fishing shallow water where the current is not too strong, a lighter line and sinker are easier to handle. For a strong current, deep or rough water, you want a heavier line. But you don't have to know any of these things. All you have to do is ask the man in the tackle shop.

If you want to buy surf-fishing gear, good rods can be purchased for $35 to $40 and reels for $20 to $35. All of it—rods, reels, line, terminal rigs, sand spikes—

can usually be bought on sale toward the end of summer. By then the fish are running good.

There is another kind of surf fishing that is utterly simple. Called poke poling, it is best done in the intertidal zone (the area between the highest high tide and the lowest low tide) of rocky coasts at low tide, when there is no large surf to knock you down. You need a bamboo pole six to ten feet long, a piece of heavy wire (like a coat hanger), and a fish hook. Attach the wire to the end of the pole by taping it down so that one end extends out a little way beyond the pole; then attach the hook, baited with mussel, abalone, squid, or such things, to the end of the wire. The fishing consists of sticking the pole down into deep pools and crevices between the rocks. Move around a bit if you haven't caught anything in a few minutes.

Take a guide to sea life with you. You may catch some odd creatures. Even if you catch *nothing*, you are still standing in a special world where you will see things no one ever saw from the beach.

The Fisherman's Catalog, Vlad Evanoff, Doubleday, New York, 1977. Superb for finding out all about the other books, equipment, facts, clubs, and everything else. Paperback.

Salt-water Fisherman's Bible, Erwin A. Bauer, Doubleday, New York. Paperback.

Surf Fishing, Vlad Evanoff, Harper and Row, New York, 1974.

Musseling

Moules à la marinière, a loaf of French bread, chilled
white wine, a green salad . . . probably no one con-
siders *that* a forgotten pleasure. But gathering the
mussels yourself may be something you hadn't thought
much about. Until a few years ago not many people in
North America, except the French-Canadians, were
interested in mussels. People who gathered anything
of the sort usually dug clams. Not so any more. Mussels have been discovered.

The best time for gathering is at low tide when the
mussels are exposed. They cling to rocks and piers and
even clumps of weeds along seacoasts everywhere. You
just pull them off. But take them only from places
washed by clear, clean, sea water. (If you don't know
the area, and you don't see anyone else taking them,
find out first if shellfishing is allowed or if it is for-
bidden because of pollution.)

Two different kinds of mussels are often found in
the same spot. The ones you want are long, oval, shiny
black, and smooth. The others have ridges and are

not recommended for eating—because they don't taste awfully good, not because they're poisonous.

You have about two hours for gathering—during which you can gather enormous amounts if you happen on a good bed. The two hours happen an hour before the tide is at its lowest and an hour afterward. Here you have a chance quite literally to watch the tide turn, to be gathering mussels and have for yourself that moment when the sea changes. Another bonus is that where there are mussels there is an area of active sea life. All sorts of other things will be there to be observed. If you are not counting on the mussels for dinner, you might find the other distractions worth all your time. If you are, come back to investigate at the next low tide.

All mussels take in a lot of sand and mud. Immediately shake out obvious dirt, rinse mussels in the sea, and put them in your bucket—with water in it. Those that feel heavier than the others might be filled with sand or mud instead of mussel. If you are uncertain whether it's mussel or mud inside, hold the shell with the opening at the top, apply pressure to the sides. A real mussel will send out a squirt of water. Mud doesn't. It doesn't do much of anything except muddy up your dinner if you miss it. Don't gather mussels unattached to something. They're dead and can be poisonous. (Never, for that matter, gather any but live shellfish for eating.)

Take your mussels home in a pail of sea water. Scrub them under running water with a brush, then, holding the mussel, grab the beard that protrudes from the closed shells and give a good yank to pull it out. (You can also scrape it off with a knife, but that seems less natural somehow.) After that, if you set them in a bucket of fresh water for an hour or two, any sand that is left will come out. The cleaner the mussels, the better (and cleaner) their broth.

Don't be surprised if otherwise nice people won't show you the location of good mussel beds. Some areas are seriously overpicked. The fact that musseling has become popular enough for *that* to happen has also caused it to come to the attention of the fish wardens. In some places musseling *might* come under clamming laws, and clamming requires a license. Licenses are a protective measure for commercial fishermen (after all, if you're getting your clams free, what happens to their catch?) and at times a protective measure for the animals, who need a little time to grow, mate, procreate, and so forth. Check at a local tackle shop if you are uncertain about regulations in your area. And if you are uninterested in eating mussels, don't gather them. Feast on the view of the sea instead.

If you come across an overpicked bed (or one where the mussels have been opened and eaten by starfish) do a little exploring. Follow inlets or streams emptying into the ocean, go back into salt marshes, dare a little off the beach track—you could discover the ultimate mussel bed. Then, of course, it's up to you whether you ever tell anyone about *your* find.

What do you need? Not much. Bare feet, a bucket, a shirt and hat to keep you from getting sunburned. (It's easy to forget about the sun with your feet in wet sand and your mind on mussels.)

Since the very act of gathering mussels, or even talking about gathering mussels, is redolent of the act of eating them, and since I started this chapter with *moules à la marinière*—it seems legitimate to talk about cooking them.

Put a cup of dry vermouth and a quarter of a cup of water in a large pot that has a tight cover. Add some chopped onions, butter or olive oil, garlic, thyme. Bring to a boil and throw in, all at once, the well-cleaned mussels. Cover the pot, keep it on a high flame, and boil the mussels for four or five minutes, or until they open. You might peek in after four minutes to check. Remove the open mussels (and throw away those that didn't open). The mussels will have rendered some juice as they steam, which adds deliciousness to the broth. Then strain the broth into bowls, one for each person, and serve each person a bowl of melted butter. Now, take your mussel by its little neck, or tail, or whatever you choose to call it, dip it into the broth, then into the butter, then into your mouth. Some people eat the neck but others say it's tough. When the mussels are gone, soak bread in the broth. When the bread is gone—well, tomorrow is another day.

Musseling is a summer activity on the East Coast, but on the West Coast it is possible only from November through April. The other six months the mussels are feeding on things poisonous to people. But West Coast winters are milder than those on the East Coast, so gathering mussels in December can still be a pleasant thing to do.

If you have an unquenchable passion for mussels you might consider living half a year on each coast.

Stalking the Blue-Eyed Scallop, Euell Gibbons, David McKay, New York, 1964. This is a book on gathering all manner of shell fish. The thorough chapter on mussels includes a variety of tasty recipes. Paper.

The Mussel Cookbook, Sarah Hurlburt, Harvard University Press, Cambridge, Mass., 1977. A hundred ways to cook a blue mussel.

Seashore Life Between Tides, W. Crowder, Dover, New York, 1975. Paperback.

Observer's Book of the Sea and Seashore, I. O. Evans, Frederick Warne, New York, 1962. Small enough to carry in a pocket and fairly encyclopedic with everything from the formation of beaches and waves to a description of the hermit crab. Hardcover.

Collecting Shells

While we're still on the beach, what about shell collecting? That's something people have done since they first set foot on beaches. Gathered for use as money, shells eventually found their way into wampum belts, an intricate, painstaking art. Gathered for use as ornament, they have been used as jewelry and in all manner of crafts. And, of course, they have always been gathered for the food—or the pearls—inside them. Even the casual beach walker, with no known interest in shells, can sometimes not resist leaning over to examine some treasure lying in the sand. But many people devote all their leisure time and vacations to shelling. Shell-collecting clubs and exhibitions are to be found throughout the country.

Like many collectors, you may at some time want to name (and label) your finds. This is one of those simple pleasures with scientific overtones that can become an all-consuming passion. The study and collection of shells is called conchology; malacology is the study of mollusks—that is, the animal inside the shell.

The best time for shelling, like musseling, is from an hour before low tide until an hour after. In the North the best season is summer, after the water has warmed up. Southern waters are the place for year-round shelling and yield the most rare and beautiful shells. They also provide the most adventurous shelling, since here many people dive for shells, coming up with magnificent specimens, not to mention the whole experience of life under water.

Shells in perfect condition, rare or not, are usually still being used as homes by living animals and must be captured, although not necessarily by diving. Most of the best shells will probably look dirty, bristly, generally unlovely. You can easily pass them up in favor of the bright, sea-gleaming shells lying in full view. But those beauties often seem to fade once they're home, while the colors of the ugly ones, protected until the moment you find them, remain.

Look for shells along coasts protected from pounding surf by headlands, offshore islands, submerged reefs, sandbars, anything that breaks the force of the waves; or where the bottom is muddy or full of seaweed or loosely bedded rocks. Look in lagoons and back bays; in the tidal pools and pockets that pit rocky coasts. Sometimes high winds toss shells up on beaches where good hunting is not usual. Look under barnacled pieces of wood, inside sponges, in the mounds of seaweed, inside large, old broken shells and cans or bottles left on the beach, at the ends of the green moss floating in tidal pools.

On some bountiful beaches you will find whole shelves of shells deposited by the tides. These are the places to station yourself in your hunting. Each wave uncovers a new layer as the shells concealing it are drawn back into the sea. Treasures are revealed, then covered. Piles of them are tossed up onto the beach, often broken, wave- and weather-beaten, but sometimes perfect as they come in on the tide: the single shells of univalves, bivalves often in perfect pairs; spirals, cones, bowls, needles, stars; stripes, speckles, dots, striations; light and dark; yellow, rose, black, purple, orange, honey-brown; luminescent colors unlike any other colors; thrown up, reached for, missed, captured by a wader farther out in the water. Need one know their names? Isn't it enough to capture? To hold?

What do you need to go shelling? Sneakers, to protect your feet from shell fragments and other rubble always under foot in good shell areas and from sting-rays and Portuguese men-of-war and other biting and stinging things; cotton work gloves, for the same reasons if you will be turning over rocks; a hat to shield you from hot sun; a bag for carrying your finds. Since many live shells are buried in the sand, you also need something for digging. Your fingers work well and are always with you, but you might want to take a small rake to uncover shallow burying mollusks, or a small shovel to uncover those hiding deeper in the sand. A knife or ice pick can be used to pry off those mollusks, like abalones, that attach themselves to rocks or pilings. A kitchen strainer works well for sifting tiny ones out of the sand; a waterscope helps you see under water without being disturbed by reflected light or ripples. The wooden buckets used by sponge fishermen, available at marine supply houses, are perfect. They have a glass area at the bottom with a diameter of a foot or more. (Or make your own—see "Make a Waterscope.")

All shells should be cleaned, but those with animals still in them *must* be, unless you have no sense of smell and live alone. There are several methods used by malacologists. Probably the most popular and least offensive is to boil the shell, then remove the animal with a circular or corkscrew motion, using something like an ice pick. The animals are easier to remove while still hot. If they are allowed to cool off they contract and parts of them can easily be left behind. You'll know about *that* in fairly short order. Bivalves —clams, mussels, and oysters—are easy to clean. They open when you pour boiling water over them, or when they are placed in carbonated water. But even boiling has its variations. Besides, not all shells should be boiled. The more exotic your shell, the more intricate the cleaning. The more intricate the cleaning, the more familiar you become with your shell.

Haven't you, after all, always imagined an intimacy with your shell?

Field Guide to Atlantic Coast Shells, Percy A. Morris, Houghton Mifflin Co., Boston, 1973. Hardcover and paper.

Field Guide to Pacific Coast Shells, Percy A. Morris, Houghton Mifflin Co., Boston, 1966. Hardcover and paper.

Seashells of North America—A Golden Field Guide, R. Tucker Abbott, Golden Press, New York, 1969.

Shell Collector's Handbook, A. Hyatt Verrill, G. P. Putnam's Sons, New York. Hardcover.

Collecting Seashells, Kathleen Yerger Johnstone, Grosset & Dunlop, New York, 1970. A well-written, enthusiastic introduction to shells and the adventure of finding them. Hardcover.

How to Clean Sea Shells, Eugene Bergeron, O. McGill, 581 Forest Avenue, Palo Alto, Calif. 94301, 1973. (You can also check with your local natural history museum or shell club about cleaning methods.)

How to Study & Collect Shells. The American Malacological Union, Inc., Rt. 2, Box 318, Marinette, Wis. 54143. A symposium on everything from collecting to cleaning to arranging a collection to lists of shell clubs and publications.

Of Sea and Shore. An informative, friendly quarterly magazine. Totally comprehensible to the beginning collector and still of interest to the most sophisticated. $5.00 a year (or $1.50 for a single issue). P.O. Box 33, Port Gamble, Wash. 98364.

A Sheller's Directory of Clubs, Books, Periodicals and Dealers. $1.50 from *Of Sea & Shore.*

Associations

The American Malacological Union, Rt. 2, Box 318, Marinette, Wis. 54143. Write to them for information on shell collecting clubs near you. They also publish an *Annual News Bulletin.*

The Conchologists of America, c/o Kathleen Daniels, Sec., Box 265 A, Route 1, Apollo, Pa. 15613. This is a newer organization. They publish a newsletter several times a year.

Shell Collections

There are some magnificent collections open to the public.

The United States National Museum (part of the Smithsonian), Washington, D.C. This is a collection with over 9,000,000 specimens, probably the world's largest.

The Museum of Comparative Zoology, Harvard College, Cambridge, Mass. About 7,000,000 specimens.

The American Museum of Natural History, 79th Street and Central Park West, New York, N.Y.

Museum of Zoology, University of Michigan, Ann Arbor, Mich. This is one of the largest collections of non-marine mollusks. (Snails, for instance, are non-marine mollusks.)

The Academy of Natural Sciences, Philadelphia, Pa.

The Delaware Museum of Natural History, Wilmington, Del.

Body Surfing

There is hardly a pleasure more elemental than body surfing. For a willingness to be carried by the sea you get your own personal chance to emerge from it. It seems downright primordial . . . the beginning of life.

Body surfing is simply making a surfboard out of your body to ride the crest of a wave as it breaks and rolls onto the sand. You must catch the wave at just the right moment for a real ride. If you are too early the wave breaks over you, or just behind you and then all you get is a shove and a dousing. If you are too late you are *in* the crest just after it releases itself and its power, and you get left behind while it rolls on to the shore without you.

The right moment is the whole thing. It is a moment most apt to happen in the Pacific where the waves are big, slow, powerful and even. They are easy to predict since they come in a regular series. But other seas will do, if the Pacific isn't immediately available.

Stand, or tread water, until you see the right wave far out, gathering momentum. Then position yourself

—swim farther out or farther in if necessary—so that you are ready to plunge toward shore in the trough created in front of the cresting wave. Once you are in the trough, swim as hard as you can. Ideally, you will be sucked down into the trough. Suddenly the cresting water above you lifts you, holds you, shoots you forward. At this moment arch, point your body with your arms like tensed wings down at your sides, flat and bulletlike. You become a missile projected by the churning, breaking wave. If it works, if you are *in,* if you *catch* the wave, you become a part of it, the forward part of the cresting wave, like the prow of a boat made somehow of churning foam, and you can ride all the way home to the sand, and come home *into* the sand like a wedge, grinding into the shore like the wave itself.

The ultimate ride sends you all the way up onto the beach, stinging from the grinding into the sand, dazed perhaps—for the space of a wave or two.

The perfect catch, the ultimate ride, the pure moment of release, of flying—it's to feel at one with the wave, in it, of it, connected to its rhythm, yet *using* its power, its locomotion, to give you the ride.

A lot of time is spent waiting for the right wave, making false starts, getting half-rides, bad rides, so-so rides. These are the ones that leave you bobbing somewhere just off shore, or the ones in which the wave chops at another wave and you get battered in between. These, of course, are part of it, part of the fun, but not the experience you dream of, that you're willing to spend an hour shivering and treading water for.

Atlantic body surfing is less dependable and less

exciting—unless it's a wild surf and you really like being tossed and battered and turned upside down. Usually it's too mild for long, rushing, rolling rides, or too wild for anything but a series of dunkings.

Even so, wherever you find a wave, try it. All of it can be good practice for that day when you will get to the ultimate Pacific wave.

Sledding on Hog Cranberry Hills

The dunes of some beaches, particularly those along the New England coast, are covered with dense mats of hog cranberries, a low, creeping shrub also known as bearberry or kinnikinick. It is abundant in northern areas of exposed rock and sand or high in the Rockies. The flowers are pink or white (or pink and white) and the berries that appear in late summer or fall are small, red, and hard. They are not good to eat (although they are among the important survival foods, should your excursion come to that). They are less bad if boiled. The leaves, dried and crumbled, make a tobacco substitute, long used by northern Indians and woodsmen.

The leaves— waxy, dark, slippery, evergreen leaves —make for some superb sledding. Just sit down on a piece of cardboard (you know, that piece of cardboard you always take to the beach with you), push yourself off and slide. Lovely slide.

Here, where a world of beach and blue, of green and flowers and warm, summer sun replaces the white world in which one usually sleds, the sensation of sliding down something is familiar, yet totally new. No layers of warm clothes, no cold, brittle air separate you from the immediacy of the slide.

But if only it were possible to find a dune high enough . . . long enough . . .

Fall

The long days dissolve, imperceptibly at first, into the first tentative reaches of fall. Here and there on green hillsides the single flame of a tree blazes red or gold. The flame catches, explodes, spreads like wildfire over the earth. The days become brilliantly clear, crisp, cloudless; flowers turn to seed; the forest floor lies newly carpeted in leaves. I feel in myself the ripeness of this season, rushing by with its swift and golden energy.

It is a bittersweet beauty that lures one out for long walks. It always seems as if it were happening for the last time, as if such glory cannot occur again. I wonder how many people suddenly find themselves philosophizing about the nature of life, come autumn. People who ordinarily have nothing to do with the outdoors drive miles to look at the leaves, while those who are rarely indoors indulge themselves with a special intensity in this best of times for almost all outdoor pleasures. Autumn is a kind of summing up. Most of the things one does in other seasons—

walking, fishing, riding, canoeing, gathering—are most special in fall when the very air makes one yearn to move, while the vast spectacle of nature encloses one within it.

A Short Walk in
Black Rock Forest

The climb up to the path junction is strewn with leaves, faded brown and golden leaves that fell early. Although they are thick enough to be slippery—and I place each foot carefully—most of them remain on the trees, clinging with all their fire till the last possible moment—crimson, orange, bright gold, and pale yellow. The gold and yellow leaves hit by the light seem pieces of the sun.

It is amazing to me that the leaves' colors have always been with them, simply covered all spring and summer, by the green, until that moment in fall when the leaf itself cuts off its access to food and water, and the colors are unmasked.

The forest floor is a continual rustle, full of scampering, busy chipmunks and squirrels. I hear a crashing sound on the slope above me and look up in time to see a deer—a doe—rushing away. She bounds a few steps, then stops to watch me—or, at least, to look at me. I stand absolutely still. Often an animal will look directly at you and, if you are totally still, it will not see you. I stand a long time, until, deciding one of us ought to move, take a step. She bounds away, now out of sight.

Deer season begins soon, and I will stay out of the forest until it's over. I wonder how my deer will fare.

Sutherland Pond, reflecting the deep blue of the autumn sky, is bluer than ever. The ducks are there. And above, lifted on the bouyant air along the hillsides, are the hawks. The trees on the steep slope leading down from Echo Rock to the pond are gold; everywhere color and scent are sharp, etched, clear, deep. There seem to be no shadows. Everything stands out, isolated.

This year's layer of cones lies scattered beneath the pines, and from the top of Black Rock the view in every direction is solid red and gold, interrupted only by the river and patches of towns. When my eye reaches the Catskills—the same distant, purple shadows they inevitably are from here—I suddenly realize I have been seeking relief from the unrelenting power of autumn.

Most exuberant, most sad of seasons—this walk has made me lonely. Suddenly a bluebird appears, perches a few feet away from me on the rock. It seems either not to know I am there or not alarmed by me. The bluebird is the bird of New York State and supposedly common in the East.

All my life I have wanted to see a bluebird.

Orienteering

Rather than being a forgotten pleasure, this one, imported from Sweden after the war, is a rapidly growing one. But it is simple. That is, simple in that it happens outdoors and requires no more equipment than a map and an inexpensive compass and anybody can do it. Very old people and little children do it. So do athletes at their peak, the United States Marines, and boy scouts. In Colorado an orienteering program has been set up for blind children using braille compasses. It is basically a competitive sport but it can just as well be a family ramble through a city park. Seasonless, it is included in fall because of the beauty of the woods and the lack of summer's heat and spring's mud.

The idea is to navigate from point to point as quickly and efficiently as possible. The number of miles and difficulty of terrain are arbitrary. They can be decided according to the skill of the participants. It is entirely in your own hands. You set up your own course. For beginners, it's best to set one up in familiar territory. A city or nearby park will do nicely. The *game* comes from planning and carrying out the fastest route over the course, something each person must do for himself.

The course must have a series of checkpoints clearly marked with flags between the start and finish—like a car rally. The participant simply marks down each checkpoint as he comes to it, before returning to the bosom of his family. As he makes his way from point to point the orienteer learns to read the landscape, becoming fully able to assess and understand it. He is continually forced to make navigational decisions. Is this straight line on the map from Checkpoint A to Checkpoint B the shortest way? What about this mountain between the two, and that rather large lake just the other side of A? Should I go around them both? It looks a long way around on the map, but it may take less time than swimming across a lake and then climbing a mountain. Etc.

The single most important piece of equipment is the map, and the prime job for the orienteer, beginner or not, is to know where he is on the map at all times. The map is properly oriented when its directions exactly correspond with directions on the ground represented by the map. If the map is *always* properly lined up, it can always be quickly consulted (although speed is less important if you are not in competition—unless, of course, night is coming on). If the map is not lined up, it is easy to go considerably off course. Lining up the map means, for instance, that if you are traveling from north to south, you would hold the map upside down. Whichever direction you are traveling, just align the easily recognizable points on the map with the actual features on the ground.

You may need to consult your compass to do this. Hold the compass at right angles to your chest. If you turn your whole body until the needle points north, rather than just twisting the compass, then, when the compass is set, you will have only to lift your eyes to be looking north. Line up the map accordingly, allowing for the difference between true north and magnetic north. Be sure, when doing this, that you are neither leaning on an iron railing nor carrying anything made of iron or steel in a breast pocket or on a belt—the smallest thing can swing the magnetic compass needle as much as ten degrees if it is near the compass. Ten degrees may not seem like much, but keep in mind that you are all alone and are trying to find your way in the woods. Looking straight down at the needle will help in precisely gauging its position.

Yes, I did say all alone. That's part of the game, although there are no rules about it, and your first time or two it might be nice to have a companion. It's more challenging alone. Besides, what if the other person makes a mistake?

The essence of orienteering is that it is a personal skill, owing nothing to outside help. I think that's why I wanted to include it in this book. Independence often seems to have become a forgotten pleasure. Exploring it outdoors, testing it, turns the exploration into a celebration of nature's spirit as well as of one's own.

There are compasses made especially for orienteering, and reading them is a lot easier than describing reading them. They are set into clear, magnifying base plates that are marked like a ruler with inches and centimeters. The needle housing is graduated into 360 degrees, and luminous points on the dial and needle make it readable at night. (In case you *were* too slow and night did, after all, come on.) Since the lines on the base plate can be matched up with the vertical lines on the map while the directional arrow sits over the transparent base plate and is therefore seen *on* the map, the whole thing really is easy to read.

Some people imagine orienteering to be a kind of treasure hunt, but it is quite definitely a game of skill and not at all a treasure hunt. Nothing is hidden. Still, the satisfaction of looking up from your map to see ahead of you the hill you expected to see; the stream, marked on the map, that is flowing down the hillside; the bridge that is supposed to be there, actually there spanning the stream; and on the bridge, the marker— is at least as great as finding treasure.

Orienteering, John Disley, Stackpole Books, Harrisburg, Pa., 1973. Mr. Disley, organizer of the first English National Orienteering Championships, tells you everything you need to know—with humor and enormous appreciation of the personal aesthetics of the sport. Included, among other things, are explanations of how to lay out a practice course and make orienteering maps, and a good description of compass practice. Paper.

The Sport of Orienteering, Stig Hedenström and Bjorn Kjellstrom, Silva Ltd., La Porte, Ind. 46350, 1977. Written specifically for Americans. Good section on map and compass.

Be Expert with Map & Compass, Bjorn Kjellstrom, Charles Scribner's Sons, New York, 1976. Mr. Kjellstrom, a former Scandinavian orienteering champion, is responsible for bringing orienteering to the United States. This book deals specifically with map and compass skills rather than with the sport of orienteering. Paper.

The Wilderness Route Finder, Calvin Rutstrum, Macmillan Publishing Co., New York, 1973. This is not an orienteering book, but if you get involved with maps and compasses through orienteering, you might want to explore the world of route-finding further. This book takes it out of the world of games, goes deeper into it, teaches it as a practical skill. Paper. $1.50.

All of these books and more (ask for their book list) are available from: The Silva Company, La Porte, Ind. 46350.

Associations

Since orienteering is not complicated but the words describing it are, the easiest way to learn is through an orienteering club—by doing. Clubs throughout the country hold meets for all levels of participants, rank beginners to experts. Even if you are not interested in anything competitive, you can still benefit from their information about local courses and maps. A list of clubs is available from The Silva Company, La Porte, Ind. 46350.

Compasses

Silva and Suunto make the most popular orienteering compasses. Each makes several models, ranging in price from about $5 to about $30. They are available at backpacking stores or from REI (see "Rafting"). Silva also makes a braille compass for the blind. Write for their catalog.

Skipping Stones

I hold the rounded, flat stone with my thumb on one edge and forefinger on the opposite. Then, low over the water, I let go, snapping my wrist to make it spin. It slaps against the water—one, two, three, four, more times—until slowing, it stays longer on the water... then too long on the water... then lets go all its speed and, piercing the water... sinks.

The stone interests me, and the process of wearing and honing wreaked by fast-moving water upon the stone until, flattened and rounded, it becomes *the* perfect skipping stone. Coming upon the pebble-strewn shore of calm water—the proper water for skipping stones—I am curious about how the stone came to that particular shore. Was the water once fast moving? Does it still move swiftly in other seasons? Does fast-moving water enter somewhere nearby?

Well, I am curious to a point... Most thought seems to wander away, dissolve into ripples, dissolve into spreading circles wherever my stone hits.

The circles stretch wider, wider, fade, merge with

the calm. They carry my mind with them. I forget about the stone. I am no longer curious. Apart from the calm water, I am no longer anything at all.

I think it's called contentment.

Gathering Nuts

Poor, absent-minded gray squirrels. They work so hard to lay in a winter's supply of nuts, gathering, storing them carefully away here and there in the ground. Then they forget where they put them. Still, I suppose they can't *all* forget . . .

Once while I was gathering nuts a gray squirrel on the next tree just sat on his branch and scolded. He may not remember where he puts his nuts, but he certainly seems to remember that they do belong to him. The entire crop, apparently.

The problem with being scolded by a squirrel is that there isn't any way to talk back to one. I considered moving on to the next tree, then decided there were nuts enough for us both. That's one of the nice things about gathering nuts—where one finds them, they are plentiful. They are also easy to gather and have so many other assets that a scolding or two seems unimportant.

Nuts are among the most nutritious of wild foods. They keep a long time. They can all be eaten raw, ground into flour to be used in bread, muffins, and such, or baked into brownies. Anybody can figure out something to do with a nut. For free, they are a tremendous bargain since they cost so much at the supermarket.

But it's easy enough to pass a nut tree without recognizing it, since the nuts in their husks look different from the nuts in their shells. Hazelnuts, for instance. The thin, hard-shelled round nut is sheathed in a sort of hairy, horn-shaped stocking. Hazelnuts grow on the West Coast and throughout the eastern half of the country on small trees (or large shrubs, depending on your point of view), in thickets, on the edges of woods, and in clearings. There are usually two nuts to a stem, but sometimes you will find just one or even three. They are ripe in the early fall, when you may well come upon a deer or a moose munching on the tree itself, while chipmunks and squirrels are gathering the nuts. I'm willing to risk a squirrel's scolding, but I'd wait until the moose was finished eating before doing any gathering of my own.

In the East and Midwest, in rich soil, you will find black walnut trees. The nuts, growing singly, in twos or threes, are encased in a round, thick, yellowish-green husk. They fall from the tree when ripe. You can remove the husk with a knife, or you can let it dry, then crack it more easily. Unless you have an immediate need for a walnut—and have a pair of gloves—it is better to let the husk dry. The fresh husks contain a brown dye that stains anything it touches—like your hands—and remains for days. (The only way to remove the stain more quickly is with a stain solvent, available at chemical supply houses.)

Butternuts are closely related to walnuts, but their

husks are different—sticky, hairy, and long rather than round. They are also less common, growing only in the Northeast—as far south as Georgia. The nuts hang in clusters of two to five, turning brown and dropping from the tree when they are ripe.

Hickory nuts are another relative of the black walnut. Growing in rich woods and bottomland, they share the East and Midwest with their cousins. There are more than a dozen kinds of hickory trees in North America. The nuts from all are edible, but some are more edible than others. A pecan, for instance, is a hickory nut supreme, but only people living in the Mississippi River Valley will find it growing wild. Next to pecans, the best of the hickory nuts are those found on the shagbark (or shellbark) hickory, which grows on hillsides, in valleys, along swamps, and in woods. It is an easy tree to identify because it looks shaggy, with its gray bark splitting into long shards that cling to the trunk. In late fall, usually after all the leaves have fallen, the husks crack open into four equal parts to reveal the smooth, ripe nut, and fall to the ground. Sometimes the nut pops entirely out.

It was a long time before I knew beechnut was something besides gum. It was, in fact, one of the most important nut foods to both Indians and early settlers. The colonists even roasted and ground it for coffee. Pretty much restricted to the East, it grows on hillsides and ridges and in rich bottomlands. The nuts, which ripen in October on their tall, bluish-gray dappled trees, usually hang in pairs, their bristly brown husks splitting open when the nuts are ripe.

One nut everyone recognizes but hardly anybody does anything about is the acorn. Many people think it's only squirrel food. Squirrels do eat it. So do birds, chipmunks, deer, sheep, and bear. And people. Acorns can be gathered from the ground beneath any of the almost forty different kinds of oak trees that spread out across the country. Every one of them is edible, but some require more work to eat than others. All acorns contain tannin, too much of which can cause stomach problems. Some acorns have too much. To make these particular acorns edible, the tannin must be leached out. This is not difficult, just time-consuming. You must shell the acorns, put them into a large pot, cover with water, and boil. Change the water as it becomes yellow (this is the tannin "leaching out"). Continue doing this until the water is no longer colored. Or, if it seems more convenient or more romantic, after shelling the nuts you can stone grind them into meal, which you place in a closely-woven cloth bag. Suspend that in the moving water of a stream for twenty-four hours.

Acorns from trees whose nuts have a low tannin content can be eaten raw or simply roasted, but you should be sure about the tree. Those from the group of oaks known as white oaks are usually sweeter, possessing less tannin, than those from the groups known as black or red oaks. Although the bark of white oaks is generally lighter than that of black or red oaks, it is not always easy to tell a white oak from a black oak. Maybe you know someone—friend, botanist, forester —in your area who can tell you where to find which.

All pines contain nuts, but the best of the edible ones come from the driest areas, particularly the Southwest, where the piñon and nut pine grow. Gathering pine nuts requires a little more patience than gathering other nuts. Unlike the fruit of other nut trees, fallen pine-nut fruit isn't of much use. The pine cones on the ground have probably already released their seeds. You must pick the still closed but ripe cones (brown, not green) from the trees. Put the cones on a screen so air can get entirely around them, allowing them to dry naturally. In a few days shake them and the nuts will fall out. (You can pick them out by pulling back each woody bract—a nice way to while away an afternoon— but it would take forever to collect any substantial amount.) Sear off the wings and husks in an open flame and either eat the clean nuts whole or grind them into a meal or flour for biscuits or cake, or grow some basil and make a *pesto* out of them.

Not nuts—but almost—are sunflower seeds. The huge sunflowers, which can grow six feet tall with flowers half a foot in diameter, are common in meadows and plains, rich bottomlands, and in waste places throughout the country. The seeds can be a nuisance to shell but are delicious to eat. Ripe in the fall, they come from the dark brown, purple, or yellow disk in the center of the flower. Collect the whole head and allow it to dry until the seeds come out easily. Then put them all in a heavy plastic or cloth bag and break the shells with a hammer or rolling pin; then empty the whole bag into a large bowl of water and stir until the seeds sink to the bottom and the shells rise to the top. Throw away the shells, roast the nuts, and sprinkle them with a little salt.

Hog peanuts grow from the East Coast through the Midwest. Their beanlike vines twine around the surrounding vegetation in cool, damp thickets and along stream banks or in rich woods. The stems are covered with long brown hairs. The leaves may or may not be slightly hairy. The vines produce two kinds of seed pods. One is above ground and looks like a flattened pea pod about an inch long. This one is *not* to be eaten. The one that *can* be eaten grows just beneath the ground, or beneath the ground cover of leaves and such. It is a rounded, fleshy pod that holds one large, light-brown peanutlike seed. These pods are just as hairy as the stems. The seeds, similar to fresh beans, can be eaten raw or cooked—the pods crack free during boiling—or they can be dried, roasted, and eaten like peanuts.

Not at all a nut, but an easily recognizable and highly prized fall food is the plump, juicy fruit of the wild rose, the rose hip. The scarlet or bright orange rose hips grow in moist open woods, fields, and meadows, along stream banks, near salt-water beaches, fencerows, and roadsides; that is, virtually everywhere except deserts. Far higher in vitamin C than an equivalent amount of orange juice, they are easy to pick, can be found far into the winter, and are, in fact, among those fruits that get juicier with freezing. They can be eaten raw or dried, but are best made into jam or a sauce.

Fall is the harvest. It is a wild one which is easy to take part in, a chance to reap without having had to sow. A couple of glorious Sunday afternoons will reward you with a winter's supply of wild foods. But do try to remember where you put them.

Edible Wild Plants, Oliver Medsger, Collier Books, New York, 1972. Pleasant and complete information about much more than nuts, but good for nuts and seeds. Provides a little information about methods of preparation, and drawings of some, but not all, plants mentioned. Paperback.

Nuts from Forest, Orchard and Field, Gray J. Poole, Dodd, Mead & Co., New York, 1974. A children's book, but helpful nonetheless.

Watching Hawks

One morning in late August as I jogged down the road along Barnegat Bay I saw a woman standing in front of the Coast Guard station with her neck craned back almost 90 degrees, field glasses at her eyes. Of course I looked up. I didn't immediately see it. But the woman saw me. "There's a peregrine falcon up there," she said, "on the aerial. They're rare."

I came back the next morning with my own glasses to find him again perched on the aerial. But now there was a second one, a young bird, perched on top of a high post nearby, picking at a breakfast of gull that lay on top of the post. The gull seemed almost alive as it was lifted up by the young falcon's beak, then dropped back upon the post. The falcon picked at it, then turned his head away and cried, repeating the procedure over and over. The first bird never left his perch but kept turning his head to look in every direction, scanning sky and bay and earth. Although he moved no more than that, one could sense his power. I saw him see the ducks in the bay, the gulls on every post and

roof and in the sky. Certainly he had already break-
fasted. The young falcon's meal was entirely his own.

The peregrine falcon is the fastest of the birds of
prey and strong and very bold. Its feet are deadly
weapons—a hit will kill a duck or a gull, yet the
peregrine falcon is only about the size of a crow.
Handsome and agile, it is a magnificent animal.

About thirteen species of hawks in the East make
their way south every autumn. There are a few more
in the West, although concentrations are rarer; the
viewing places are in the East and Midwest. Migration
begins in late August, with a peak between mid-Sep-
tember and mid-October. Most of the hawks going all
the way south head for Texas, where the end of
October is signaled by the coming of thousands and
thousands of birds.

But non-Texans can also have extraordinary views.
The most spectacular migration occurs at Hawk Ridge,
in Duluth, Minnesota. Hawk Mountain, Pennsylvania,
is another major viewing site, although one is apt to
see half the number of birds one could see at Hawk
Ridge. There are other special places and organized
hawk watches as well. (For more information, see end
of chapter.)

Since the birds do not follow an exact schedule, you
may arrive at a sanctuary and see only a few. Or you
may see thousands. Some, the broadwings particularly,
fly in huge groups. There can be thousands of them
swirling up in a thermal together, simply swirling and
swirling, mixing and crisscrossing and swirling upward
until one glides out and away, followed by the next
and the next and finally, in a long, long line, by the
others.

Exuberant, playful, triumphant—the movement is an unconscious ceremony performed by these masters of the air, over and over forever.

The View from Hawk Mountain, Michael Harwood, Charles Scribner's Sons, New York, 1973. An informative and wonderfully written book that will probably involve you with every hawk you ever see for the rest of your life. It also contains a good bibliography, should you want to read further. Hardcover.

Watching

A few other hawk-watching places:

Hook Mountain State Park, overlooking the Hudson in Upper Nyack, N.Y.

Montclair Quarry, N.J.—a sanctuary run by the New Jersey Audubon Society.

Cape May, N.J.

Check your local Audubon Society (see "Watching the Birds Come Back") for still others.

For information about organized hawk watches throughout the country, write: The Society for the Preservation of Birds of Prey, Box 891, Pacific Palisades, Calif. 90272.

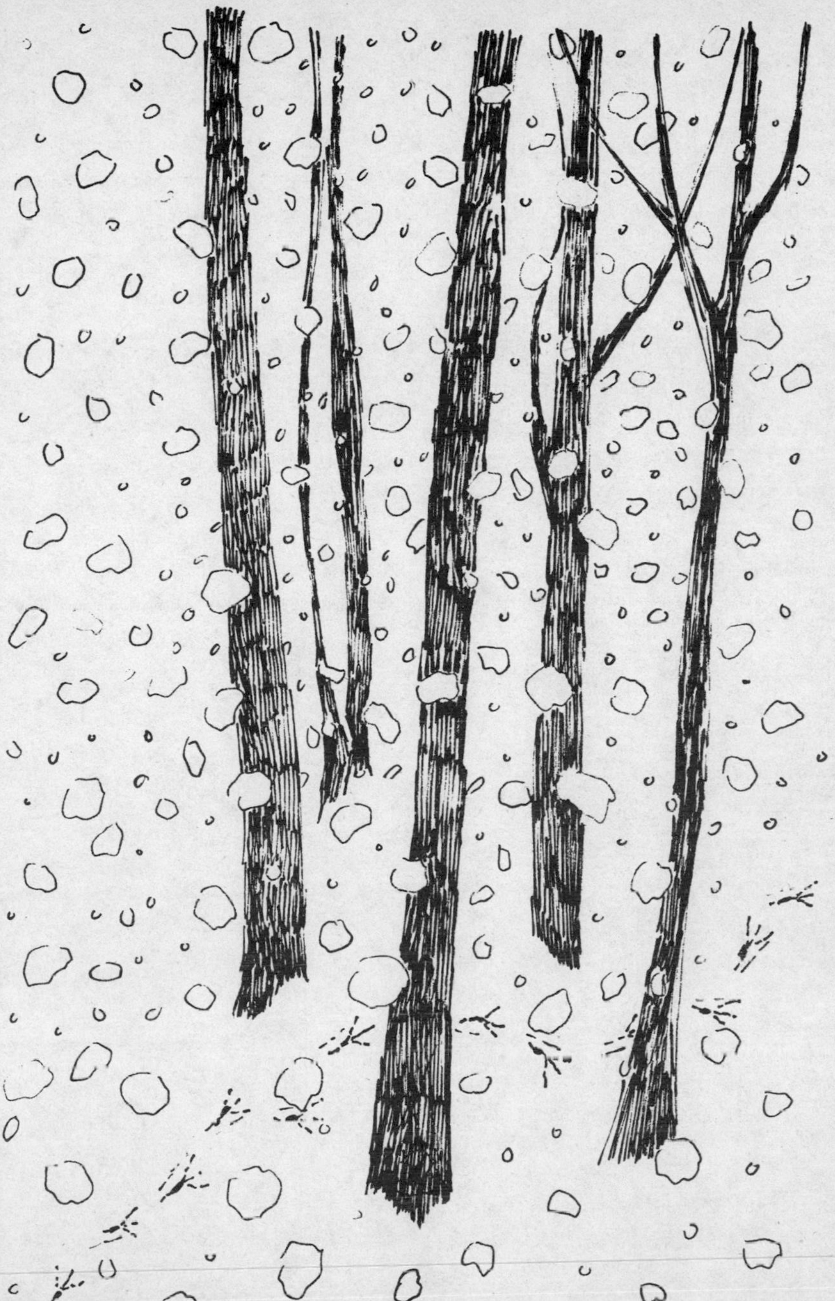

Winter

Gaunt bare trees stand gray against the gray, snow-portending sky. The softness of new snow holds the silence of the months of snow. I come upon the footprints of a rabbit, a fox, a moose. Brushing aside the snow beneath evergreens, I am rewarded with a find of plump, red, juicy wintergreen berries. I reach the open space of a snow-hidden lake, its vast life slowed but continuing under the ice, all of it now the province of a solitary ice fisherman.

One of the greatest pleasures of winter—sitting in front of a roaring fire with a glass of brandy, a good book, a loyal old dog at your feet—is even greater if you've gone outside first: a tramp in the woods, along a canal, down a country road, across a city park; a morning spent ice fishing or skating on a woodland pond, or searching for winter foods, or following the tracks of an animal over otherwise untracked snow, lacing on a pair of snowshoes or cross-country skis where the snow is deep; sliding down the hills of the nearest park on a tray, a sled, a toboggan, anything that comes to hand. Unlike other seasons, winter offers no automatic invitation outside. Effort is involved. To get from warmth to the outdoors you must crash through barriers. Well then, crash them. Enter deep, wild, merciless, spellbinding beauty, the end of the year with all stops out.

A Short Walk in
Black Rock Forest

The steep trail up from Mine Hill Road into the forest
is icy under the snow but not long, and there are rocks
enough jutting out from their snow cover to grab on to
when my foot slips. At the top of the trail I have, once
again, a view through the leafless trees across the
valley to Schunemunk, to sky all the way to the Catskills. I turn left to follow the trail over Sackett
Mountain.

The stream is covered by ice, but in some places I
can hear the water rushing underneath. Sometimes,
near the stream's edge, a thin layer of ice, the kind
that is fun to step on and hear the cracking, and see
the delicate cracks spreading out to the edges of the
ice, covers brown leaves. The edges of the leaves
and the cracks in the ice make a picture like an ab-
stract painting worked over and over to make layers
of paint.

It is easy in winter to know everything that is
happening in the forest. Everybody's trails can be fol-

lowed. Now I come upon the footsteps of a deer, then a rabbit. The snow, crusty on top, breaks through now and then and I plunge in deep, leaving behind me a crater of a footstep. The same thing has happened with the deer. Suddenly I come upon a man's footsteps entering from another trail. He has gone the direction I am going. They are fresh steps, not yet blown by wind or melted and stretched by the sun, not yet settled into the snow but still on top of it all. He too is alone. (I assume it's a man. It has awfully big feet, and there have been no reports of yetis in the area.)

I follow his footsteps, often stepping in them since they are more solid than the surrounding snow, as I continue past the ruins of the log cabin toward the road. I find myself—at the same moment—both glad to know there is another person in the forest and resentful at finding human footsteps in the path. Is life such an ambivalence for other people? Sometimes in one of those moments when it seems necessary to define Life (you know those moments . . .) the definition comes out something like: Life is a fork in the road where one must continually take both forks at once. It's a definition guaranteed to remove any possibility of movement.

Fortunately, at the road, his tracks turn the opposite direction from mine. By the time I reach Echo Rock I am warmed enough by the slight uphill walk to enjoy sitting there a while, my poncho beneath me on the top part of the snow-covered rock. From here the pond looks quite frozen, while the white hills around the pond seem to stretch, pure and silent, all the way to New York, there to be replaced by silver towers.

The gentle path to the pine woods is crusty and the

walk takes longer than in other seasons, although in the pines there seems to be less snow than elsewhere.

The uphill to Black Rock is an effort. In some spots the snow is deep, in others completely blown off, exposing ice. I make my way around each patch of ice, once again grabbing on to any piece of rock that offers itself. On top most of the snow is blown off and the wind is fierce. I hardly take the time to look at the view, although I am aware of the white Catskills far against the distant sky. I quickly cross over to the back of the mountain, to my sheltered niche and one more lovely lunch in the sun atop—or rather, almost atop—Black Rock.

Sledding

I can remember settling down on my Flexible Flyer, poised at the top of the backyard, hands firmly grasping the steering mechanism, giving myself a push, and zooming off, down the sloping snow-deep yard into the field behind the house. Things were simple in those days. A sled was a sled, a kid's toy except when the snow got too deep and it could be used to haul wood or groceries. Before I was a teenager the sled had already been consigned to the woodshed, never to be considered again, except while watching *Citizen Kane,* when, of course, it took on enormous proportions. One day, as an adult, I visited some other adults a short way out of the city who had decided to spend the day sledding.

It was a sunny Sunday and we packed sandwiches and thermoses of hot chocolate into our rucksacks, then set off for a nearby park with wide open hills, dragging two sleds behind us. When we reached the top of what they considered a suitable hill it suddenly occurred to me what I was about to do. It wasn't the angle of the hill. I ski hills far steeper. It had something to do with the angle of me. Things look different if you are standing up on skis or lying head down on your belly. Besides, hadn't I watched sledding at the Winter Olympics? It was not for no reason that sledding was an Olympic sport! The sound of speed and the blur of the single-man luge swooping up the curving bank of a fast, steep course filled my head, careened through my soul to be replaced—without stopping—by the utter, flying, irrevocable speed of the two-man and four-man bobs. I decided not to be first. Actually, I thought I'd stay on top and prepare lunch.

But everyone else went, laughing, speeding down the hill—singly, sitting in pairs, lying one on top of the other, head first on their stomachs, feet forward on their backs as in the luge. How long could I hold out? There wasn't, after all, just the afternoon to be gotten through. *Their* evening would be full of the day's triumphs. But mine . . . ?

I was hardly aware of climbing onto the sled until suddenly all I knew was speed, immense speed, a fast wind made all of white, close to the ground, movement uncontrollable and yet without question controlled; the sheer, white, glittering speed of it! And again and again, each time believing that *this* time the sled would not run out on the long flat at the bottom of the hill, but would soar farther and farther, leaping stone walls, flying down hills no one had yet imagined. . . . I began the trudge up for yet another ride.

What interested me, finally, on my last way up, was that the rides had elicited no childhood memories whatsoever. The experience was entirely new. It was as if I had never seen a sled before.

In fact, because I had never really looked, I never *had* seen sleds like those I now began to see: metal discs (Flexible Flyer made those too, before they went out of business), plastic circles, and short plastic tobogganlike shapes, trays, the tops of garbage cans, inner tubes, anything and everything that was low enough and would slide.

My street ends at the top of a steep hill in the park. The minute a new snowfall stops, that hill must have more sleds per inch on it than any hill in America. It doesn't take long for the snow to get packed down into the slickest, fastest track *any* side of Lake Placid. When that happens, the smallest children head a few streets south with their sleds, to the shorter, fluffier hills in the park. The big hill becomes the province of daredevil teenagers by day—and adults by night.

Now and then an adult will grab a little extra sledding. One morning I saw a woman with a sled walking her two dogs. That is, the dogs were standing at the top of the hill watching, as she sailed down on her sled, hauled it up again, sped down again, and so on and on. Remarkably patient dogs, but I suppose they thought it was nice she could get out to play now and then.

Sledding seems to me a kind of perfect sport. It provides the thrill of speed and the superb exercise of walking back up the hill. Certainly I have never seen an activity more democratic. Anything can be used and it can be done wherever there is snow—as easily in the city as in the country and, for that matter, on flat land as well as on land that slants.

In flat land you can harness a sled to a horse. (Skiing behind a horse is common in the prairie states. Nothing says you can't substitute a sled for skis.) I have had only one experience of harnessing an animal to a sled. It was a reindeer in Finnish Lapland. He stood quietly while I settled myself in the canoe-shaped sled, my legs stretched out in front as I leaned against the back. (The sled provides one with a rather odd view, since the *only* thing you see is the back end of the reindeer.) I pulled a warm blanket over my legs, took hold of the reins and prepared myself for a long ride. The reindeer took off like an explosion, raced to a curve in the road, headed directly into the curve, swerved at the last possible minute, swerved fast. The sled turned over and I fell into the snowbank. (He obviously had a certain amount of experience with this.) It was exciting sledding, although I have not been left with an overfondness for reindeer. You might try to find an agreeable horse.

A Few of Winter's Foods

You may have picked, in other seasons, parts of some winter food plants. Their appearance will have changed in winter. So will most gathering techniques, since now you will at least have to root around a little beneath the snow, if not actually dig—a process that will keep you warm.

Arm yourself with a guidebook, or a friend who knows wild foods, a digging tool, and a thermos of something hot; then head out to the nearest fields. You won't have to go far. Many of winter's plants are partial to the cleared sides of roads. (The roots— which is what most of the winter foods are—are not subject to the same kind of road pollution as are the leaves.)

If you find the vine of the wild potato along the roadside, dig down for the root. It looks much like a yam. You could have to do some serious digging since the vertical roots are sometimes huge. Look for the evening primrose in the same place. The roots can be boiled or roasted as you would a potato. Near these two you may also find chicory. Roasted and ground, chicory roots have long been used either as a coffee substitute, or added to coffee, both to stretch and to flavor it.

Did you find lamb's quarter in the spring? If you can remember where, go back in early winter and gather the seeds. They can be ground into flour, or boiled to make a cereal.

Everybody recognizes cattails. Their starch-rich roots can be ground into flour, while the part of the plant at the top of the root can be eaten raw or cooked —again, like potatoes. While you're gathering cattails, if the water they are near is not yet frozen, see if you can find yellow pond lilies. (The flowers, of course, will be long gone.) The roots are another potato substitute. Look for arrowhead in the same, damp place. Dried, it can be ground into flour.

Ground nut is a vine easily found in winter. It turns very white as it twines about the plants in thickets, along streams or other low ground. Its tuberous root has a long history as a staple food (yet another potato substitute) of eastern American Indians and early settlers.

I mentioned the hog peanut in the section on nuts. Look for it in winter too. The seed was an important winter food for midwestern Indians.

The leaves of the Labrador tea plant, a shrub that grows in cold bogs and forests in the northernmost parts of the United States and in Canada, dried in the sun or over a slow flame, are used for (oddly enough) tea.

The roots of the catbrier, a vine that climbs on trees or woodland brush—mainly in the southern states

—provides a substitute for gelatin. Like Jell-O, it can be used to make a flavored drink. Combined with sassafras root, which you will find in dry woods and along roadsides, and yeast and sugar, it makes root beer. Sassafras root bark can be dried and used for tea or as a cinnamonlike spice. (I read somewhere recently that sassafras root is *suspected* of being a carcinogen. But then, so it seems, is life.)

After frosts, and the more frosts the better, the fruit of the mountain ash, a small tree (or large shrub) that grows in woods, on rocky slopes, and along roads, can be picked. It is a red-orange cluster of berries— delicious stewed and sweetened, or in pies and jams.

Frosts improve a lot of things. Wintergreen, for instance. The more these charming little red berries freeze, the plumper and juicier they become. They are wonderful raw—to nibble as you walk—or added to pancakes or muffins. You'll find them by rooting around a bit in the snow, particularly beneath evergreen trees. The leaves of this low, creeping plant can also be nibbled, steeped to make tea, made into wine or beer, or used as a medicine, similar to aspirin.

Highbush cranberry is another berry that improves with freezing. It grows along shores, on rocky slopes, and in cool woods. Too sour to be eaten fresh, the berries can be cooked with sugar into a cranberry sauce, made into a jelly, or boiled with sugar and lemon or orange peel—with a little of the orange juice thrown in—to make a drink very high in vitamin C. (Strain the juice and dilute it with water before drinking it.)

Cassina and inkberry are evergreen holly plants that grow mainly in the Southeast. Cassina berries are red, inkberries black. The dried leaves of both plants are used for tea and, unlike most tea substitutes, contain caffein.

If you can't find *any* of these things—or the others I haven't mentioned but that you will come across in wild food guides (see "A Lunch of Spring")—there *is* one perfectly marvelous winter food that no one in snow country can possibly not find.

Snow. Made into snowballs and served in a dish with maple syrup poured over them—unquestionably one of the great pleasures of winter.

Tracking

Last April I drove up to the Catskills to spend a couple
of days hiking. Two days earlier a freak snowstorm
had deposited several inches of snow in New York
City and more upstate. But this morning was brilliantly
clear, with a warm, strong sun and not a sign of snow
in town. It had gone as suddenly as it came. I never
even considered how much might be left in the mountains. Suddenly I saw them from the road as I drove
through a valley already fully green. Snow-covered,
as if they were Alps at the very least, they looked
higher, far higher, than they had ever been. I could
hardly wait to reach them.

There was almost two feet of snow there. The day
following the storm—yesterday—had been gray and
cold. On my trail, which followed the escarpment overlooking the Hudson Valley, there were small patches
of clear rock where today's sun hit the exposed ledge,
but where the trail curved back into the shadow of the
woods, the snow had hardly begun to melt. I found
myself frequently sinking into it, almost to my knees.

Each time I slowly pulled myself free. The snow was wet and heavy, and lifting a foot from it was work, frustratingly slow. No need to rush, I kept saying to myself. Plenty of light left and you're not going awfully far. It was then I noticed the bear tracks.

This was the same general area where I had seen the dead bear in the cave last summer. I had planned, in fact, to return to camp via the trail past that cave. Maybe it was, after all, not dead. I looked closely at the tracks, trying rather hard to decide they belonged to a dog. I carefully checked them out in the field guide to tracks I carry in my pack all winter. There is no way to make the tracks of a bear look like those of a dog, no matter how much you squint or look sideways or otherwise evade the issue.

It may sound as if I were not excited about having discovered the track. I was. One of the things that interests me especially about hiking in winter is the possibility of coming across somebody's tracks and figuring out whose. But where I ordinarily hike in winter the tracks belong to deer or rabbit or fox. I was a little uncertain how I felt about following the bear's trail through snow that kept such close hold of me. But I felt encouraged by the fact that I was following his tracks rather than the other way around. I would have liked seeing him, except that I thought he might be a bit put out by the late snow, grumpy about not easily finding whatever it was he'd already started on as his spring diet. I wondered if he would enjoy a peanut butter sandwich, then supposed he would. Peanut butter and honey—what bear could resist that? I considered turning around but decided that was a hysterical gesture and continued on. When

I first lost the track I was relieved . . . until relief gave way to the thought that now, of course, the bear was lurking somewhere there in the spruce forest. *That* thought made me even more relieved when I picked up his tracks again.

All along this route are shallow shelters and caves formed by rocks. I investigated them all—from a slight distance—as I approached. They seemed singularly free of bears. Somewhere shortly before the junction with the path on which I had found last summer's bear cave I ran out of tracks. I looked carefully for some at the junction. There were none. No reason a bear has to follow the path *all* the way, I thought. He could easily go cross country. He is obviously waiting in his cave.

I began my walk down that path. This area, one of the few places in this part of the Catskills where there is ever any water at all, remains damp even in late summer. Now, with all the snow and snow melt, it was a swampland. Where the snow did not come up to my knees, the water came over them. I found myself often balancing on twigs, leaping from occasional tufts of solid snow to piles of sticks to exposed rock to twigs; jumping a fast, deep, and cold stream, slightly too wide for me to jump, but I'd be damned if I intended to fall in.

I forgot about the bear. At the bottom of the trail I realized I hadn't even seen last summer's cave. Of course, I also hadn't actually seen much of the trail. I felt quite pleased that I hadn't turned back upon seeing the tracks.

The tracks animals leave in snow may be the easiest to identify, although you will find tracks in mud, sand, dust, and anything else soft enough. But the sheer drama of life in winter makes tracking then particularly fascinating. Besides, on a nice winter day in the wilds—or in your backyard or city park—there are fewer distractions than in other seasons.

Through their tracks it is possible to discover shy or cautious animals you may not have known were in your area. You might become a witness to an event in an animal's life, without ever seeing the animal. You come upon rabbit tracks, for instance. Then, suddenly, there is another set of tracks—fox or coyote. The pattern of the rabbit changes. The rabbit darts, turns. The pursuer is hard on his heels . . .

Did the rabbit escape? Are those the tracks of a third animal who somehow joined in? What animal? Why did he join? Are those drops of blood?

Fresh tracks, of course, are easiest to identify. Sun on the snow affects tracks, as it melts the snow and the track spreads out. But even fresh tracks can be confusing. The entire track may not exist if the ground is irregular or if all the toes do not show. The track pattern changes with a change in the animal's gait. Sometimes the hind feet are behind the front feet, sometimes before.

Even so, you can usually determine the general type of animal. If you find only toe marks, the track belongs to an animal that moves quickly—either to capture its dinner or to avoid being someone else's. Tracks showing the whole foot are likely to be those of animals not so much in need of speed, like skunks, porcupines, and bears. If you find well-developed claw marks, the animal is probably one that climbs trees or digs. Some animals drag their tails in snow (but not in mud, sensible creatures that they are). Some, like the fox, drag their tails only when trey're tired. Imagine going out for a winter walk with a friend and being able to say, "Aha, Nathaniel, we are on the trail of a tired fox!"

Tracking may get you near an animal, but to get close enough really to observe it, you may have to do a little stalking. Animals depend chiefly on their senses of smell and hearing for protection. Some have sharp eyesight. Some, like moose, are nearsighted. What most see is movement, not details. (You will see more animals if you use the same technique—looking for movement first, details later.) To stalk an animal you want to evade its senses. If you come toward it with the wind in your face (i.e., downwind of it) you have a good chance of getting close without alerting it to your presence. Should you somehow come upon it from the upwind side without alarming it, make a semicircle around it before getting closer. Use any available cover —stumps, rocks, big trees, culverts—if you want to continue watching it.

(You can tell which way the wind is blowing on a still day by wetting a finger and holding it up. The side toward the wind will be cooler.)

Stay off crunchy snow and dry twigs or leaves. Your footsteps make no sounds on light snow or soft ground. If the animal discovers you, stop dead still. It may look around to see what's there. It might even look directly at you. If you are completely still it may look at you and not see you, then settle down again to do whatever it was doing.

You have the greatest chance of coming across animals at night, when many are most active. Following tracks in the light of a full moon on the snow is both

easy and highly evocative. It can also be heartrending
if the snow is deep and soft (and you are on snowshoes or skis) and you come upon a deer or fox floun-
dering. There is nothing you can do about this except
watch; maybe learn how to deal with deep snow . . .
although the chief lesson is probably that if you are
without snowshoes or skis, you might forgo deep snow.
Most animals with a choice will. Deer, for instance,
will use any available path in the snow since paths are
apt to have hardened enough to keep them from sinking far in. They will gladly follow the path you've
made. Who then is tracking whom?

A Field Guide to Animal Tracks, Olaus J. Murie,
Houghton Mifflin Co., Boston, 1975. *The* field guide—
but also a lovely book to read if animals interest you,
even if you never look at a track. Hardcover and
paper.

Whose Track Is It? Richard Headstrom, Ives Wash-
burn Inc., New York, 1977. Hardcover.

Snowshoeing

Is it possible to feel a nostalgia for a sport 6000 years old? Actually, snowshoeing hasn't been a sport *all* that time. For about the first 5900 years it was a practical means of locomotion in snow country, used by foresters, soldiers, farmers, assorted travelers, and occasional horses. The horses wore a round snowshoe on each hoof.

The recent resurgence of interest has occurred mainly because snowshoes are so useful to winter hikers and backpackers. In the unbroken, uneven snow of the backcountry, they are more manageable and less risky in case of a fall than skis. They are also lighter to carry when the terrain becomes walkable again. This use of them, though, takes on a kind of seriousness not so much present on excursions in the nineteenth and early twentieth centuries, when people simply put snowshoes on to go out for a walk to the neighborhood inn.

In those days, a snowshoe hike on a full-moon night

became a gala event. Huge groups of snowshoers gathered in town for a tour out into the countryside. Under the glittering cold brilliance of the moon in the sharp, clear air, they traveled over snow-covered hills and back roads, through forests and across farms to come—always at just the right moment, of course—to the inn. Warm light spilling out of the windows announced the coziness of a rustic room where dinner was laid and waiting.

In New England, morning outings for breakfast were also popular then. The supplies were pulled on a sled, and a huge and warming breakfast fire was built in the snow. Since nothing equals a New England breakfast under *any* circumstances, what could be more perfect?

Snowshoeing is simple. It gears itself to *your* pace, not the other way around. Everybody can do it. It is, indeed, an activity for whole families or communities. Or for someone who wants to be alone.

The shoes feel a little awkward at first—as any extension of your body would—but it doesn't take many steps before you get the knack of it. You needn't worry about having to keep a tremendously wide stance, the common concern of beginners. To move forward, simply lift one foot and pass it over the standing shoe. Then avoid putting it down on top of that shoe, since moving is difficult if one foot is standing on top of the other.

You can try it in your own backyard. There is probably a pair of old snowshoes left over from the 1930s hanging up, somewhere, in the garage or attic of somebody you know. They may not be the perfect kind, but they'll do to try out this adventure. If they have been long unused, check their condition. If the finish seems worn and dry, cover them with a coat of waterproof spar varnish, which will keep the rawhide lacing from getting wet from the snow and loosening. (Chances are, if you are finding snowshoes long stored, they *will* have rawhide lacing rather than Neoprene, which is often used now. Neoprene does not require varnishing. Also check to make sure the rawhide hasn't been nibbled by mice, or it could just come apart as you start across the yard.) The snowshoes will probably have some sort of binding attached to them. If their owner cannot explain this binding to you, you will have to figure it out yourself. None of them are very complex. Just remember that it's there to keep your foot on the snowshoe. Wear soft shoes like high moccasins with several warm pairs of wool socks, or a snowmobile boot, or any other boot you might have whose bottom will be easy on the lacing. Lug-soled hiking boots can be fairly rough on lacing (although, obviously, winter hikers and mountaineers who will not be continuously on their snowshoes wear them). You might find it easier to start out using ski poles to help your balance, but you can do without them too.

You can rent snowshoes in some ski shops for a few dollars a day. This is probably the ideal way to try them before deciding to buy, since you will be able to rent whatever type is best for the local terrain and snow conditions. If you are planning an outing beyond your backyard or the park down the street, take along a pocket knife and a few pieces of rawhide thong to make any repairs that might be needed. You'll be able to figure those out too. The snowshoe is a primitive implement.

It was the advent of downhill skiing in the thirties that pushed snowshoeing into the realm of nostalgia. Snowshoeing was largely abandoned as recreation and became, once again, the province of the people whose work takes them out into the backcountry in winter— virtually the same people who have used snowshoes for 6000 years.

In their current renaissance they are, for sure, a great boon in deep snow, whether you are foraging, tracking, or simply out for a hike. But wouldn't it be nice to recapture some of that nineteenth-century spirit of just plain fun? The most difficult part will be to find a suitable inn . . .

But that kind of exploring is adventure too. You might do a little investigating before your excursion. If no inn is available, it's quite likely you will be able to make arrangements for dinner with a farm family. In small towns, ask about such a possibility in a sporting goods store. (They are used to dealing with hunters and fishermen who also like to eat.) Or ask at a small grocery that would, in season, sell the produce of local farmers.

Then check the paper for the next full moon.

The Snowshoe Book, William Osgood and Leslie Hurley, The Stephen Greene Press, Brattleboro, Vt.

05301, 1975. This is a complete and charming guide to history, equipment, and technique. Easy to read and immensely useful. Paper.

Snowshoeing, Gene Prater, The Mountaineers, 719 Pike St., Seattle, Wash. 98111, 1975. A good book on equipment and technique. Paper.

Snowshoeing Hikes in the Cascades and Olympics, Gene Prater, The Mountaineers. A guide to 81 hikes; contains useful information on snowshoes as well. Paper.

Skating on a Woodland Pond

We packed hotdogs and marshmallows and thermoses of hot toddy, wrapped ourselves in the warmest clothes possible, grabbed kindling and a dry log each from the woodpile, slung our skates over our shoulders, and headed down the snow-covered path. Then we turned around and headed back *up* the path—we had forgotten to bring a broom.

From the cabin it is less than a quarter of a mile to the rocky point that juts out into the lake. The point was covered by soft new snow, and we would never have known where the point ended and the lake began if not for the large, upright rock a few feet out into the lake from the point. Now the rock indicated where our ice began.

We arranged the logs so we could quickly start the fire when we were finished skating. Meanwhile, the best skater among us took upon himself the job of sweeping the snow from the ice. Gracefully and quickly, he cleared a large area of the lake. The ice itself was hardly as smooth as the ice of artificial rinks, but it wasn't bad, with only occasional hairlines veining it.

Leaving our warm parkas to put on later, we set off after the sweeper. He still had the broom with him and, as he continued across to the other side, he looked as if he were waltzing with a very thin lady.

The lake is surrounded by evergreen-covered hills. On the side where the cabin stands are a few other houses; otherwise, nothing. As we skated across from the point, our view was of forested hills and sky, the graying sky of winter late afternoon, almost the color of ice, gray-white ice. Even the sun hung like a gray-white ball.

Except where it had been cleared, the lake itself was defined only by its flat bareness, its whiteness rising into white banks that rolled back into the hills. The dark shapes of the trees were softened by their cover of new snow.

We skated back and forth across the lake. It gave us a great sense of traveling somewhere on skates each time we approached the far shore. (Some of us approached it a little more gracefully than others of us, but we all had the same sense.) By the time we skated back to the point for the last time it was almost dark. We lit the fire, which flared, caught, and was immediately warming. Snuggled into our warm jackets, we attached hotdogs to sticks, poured ourselves hot drinks, sat (very close together) on our thick wool blanket, and settled down to a dinner that never tasted *that* good in summer.

Any woodland lake or pond that freezes solid can become your own special, private rink. Here you have the pure fun of ice skating combined with the adventure of making your own space and the intimacy of nature. It is only essential to *know* that the ice is solidly frozen.

How do you know? You can automatically assume that ice in narrow channels, or next to piers, bridges, trestles, rocks, and stream inlets or outlets, or ice above springs coming up from the bottom is unsafe. Gray spots on otherwise white ice are signs of springs from the bottom. Stay away, too, from river ice— unless its thickness is a known fact—since moving water doesn't usually freeze well enough for skating.

Two to four inches of good ice is considered the minimum safe thickness. The best ice—tough and elastic—is that formed early in the season. But early season ice that is *just* safe in the morning can become dangerous as the day warms up. A lovely, warm sun can also wreak havoc on even properly thick ice once the ice has been exposed to most of a winter's worth of weathering.

Judging clear and flawless new ice requires a little effort since you cannot *see* its thickness. Try kicking through with the heel of your skate. If you can, it's too thin. If you can't, test it further by walking out on it— very slowly and over shallow water. If one foot breaks through while the other is (you hope) still on something solid, you can also figure it's too thin. Carry an ice chisel or ax and cut out pieces of ice to measure at frequent intervals. Cover the entire area on which you plan to skate. Do this with a rope-carrying companion a short distance *behind* you.

By far the simplest way to find out about ice is to ask local people who know the lake. If there are any. When your goal is a woodland pond, requiring a short walk to reach, you may not find anyone around who knows, although local papers sometimes report ice conditions for the benefit of fishermen. If you happen to come upon a few ice fishermen right there *on* the ice, it's safe enough for you too. Just be careful of fishing holes—manned or abandoned.

Of course, you might have your own method for testing ice. A friend of mine tests the ice in his pond by driving his jeep out onto it. Last winter the jeep sank.

The ice on lakes will not always be ideally smooth— it hardly ever is. That flawless new ice is subject to many pressures. Different rates of freezing for different parts of the lake, thawing, refreezing, buckling, and a slew of other things cause naturally made ice to have very varying surfaces. It might help your skating to keep in mind that the perfection you seek is not so much of ice, but of nature.

About learning to ice skate: You might find it easiest (least unstable) to skate with a companion who knows how. Cross your arms in front and hold both your companion's hands. He or she should have one arm in front of you, one circling behind your back. Or you might try skating with a broom. Push it before you for support. (But do it on ice someone else has already cleared.) Or try skate-sailing (see next chapter), a superb way to learn, since the sail and the wind will support you.

Make sure your skates are evenly and firmly laced so your ankles are well supported—but not so tight that circulation is cut off. If your ankles seem wobbly no matter what you do, this may not be the sport for you.

Children don't need skates to skate, but can manage on their boots. But they (the children, not the boots) should be well padded—perhaps nicely surrounded by a couple of pillows, held in place at waist or hip level with a belt or rope.

Skate-Sailing

Half person, half sail, you and your sail become a new being, born to ride the wind, effortlessly gliding at twice the speed of wind. Like soaring, or skiing down a long, long mountain in an endless series of perfectly linked turns, the feeling of skate-sailing is one of ultimate grace.

Skate-sailing can be done on ice too rough for ordinary skating, and you need be neither an experienced skater nor a sailor to try it. The skating part is easy since both feet stay on the ground at all times and you've got the sail to hold on to. Proper handling of the sail is not difficult either, once you can make yourself remember to lean on it. What you are actually leaning on is the wind. Trust it. It will, indeed, hold you up.

The traditional sail consists of 50 to 60 square feet of cloth, tightly stretched over a cross-frame of light spars (the rounded wood or metal supports for sail rigging; boom and mast are spars). The sail forms a rectangle broader at the top than at the bottom. It is carried between the wind and yourself, with the boom—the middle spar—resting on your windward shoulder. Your hand on the same side grabs the mast just below the boom. The other hand remains free. The sail will stay securely on your shoulder, held by the pressure of the wind. Meanwhile, keep your feet fairly close together, with the right foot a little ahead if the sail is held on your right shoulder, your left foot if on the left shoulder. Your body should be straight and quite rigid, leaning against the sail. As the entire sail tilts into the wind, every ounce of the wind's power is used to drive you forward.

But it is *you* who are in full control, and you can stop when you please. If you lift the sail into a horizontal position over your head while you face directly into the wind it will float out behind you (still over your head) and you will stop. Use the same motion to turn, circling into the wind as you lift the sail and allowing yourself to coast around while gradually switching the position of your feet. Once you are facing the new direction, simply lower the sail onto the other shoulder.

The techniques are simple and, because of the stability lent by the sail, spills are infrequent and rarely serious in spite of the speed. The angle at which you strike the ice will merely send you sliding. While skate-sailing does not require great strength (children and small women can manage as easily as men), it does develop fast reflexes and good coordination.

If you are already a skater, whatever kind of skates you normally use will work fine for you. If you have a choice, racing skates are best since they provide the most directional stability. Hockey skates are next best.

But whatever you use, the blades must be sharp.

As for the sail, you can make your own or you can purchase one (see end of chapter).

Dress for warmth and ease of movement. Two pairs of wool socks are essential. *You* are protected from the wind by the sail, but your feet can get colder skate-sailing than just plain ice skating. They don't have much to do for skate-sailing. If they are cold before you even put on your skates, run a little; then make sure the skates are evenly laced from the toes up. (That is, don't make them tighter at the ankle for support.) If your feet get too cold while sailing, put the sail down and simply skate a little. Even if you don't know how to skate, the *effort* will make use of your feet. If they're too cold for that, and you're on the opposite side of a large lake from the warm boots you left on shore, take off your skates and run in place on the sail. This won't help the sail a lot, but it will do wonders for your feet.

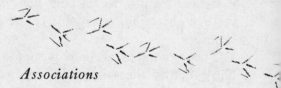

Associations

Plans for making skate-sails ("Practical Suggestions for Making and Using Skate-Sails") are automatically sent to you if you join the Skate-Sailing Association of America. Membership costs $2 a year dues, plus a $1 initiation fee. You also get—as long as there are copies left—a marvelous and charming booklet called *Skate-Sailing* by R. C. Jefferson.

For more information about membership write: Commodore Basil Kamener, Skate-Sailing Association of America, 4 Manor Road, Livingston, N.J. 07039; or Commodore Ralph Albrecht, Skate-Sailing Association of America, Mid-West Division, 6021 Old Auk Road, Madison, Wis. 53705.

Ready-made sails cost from $80 to $90. For information about them, write: Al Goldberg, Waterfun, 323 Four Brooks Road, Stamford, Conn. 06903.

A simpler form of sail can be made with whatever is at hand. For instance, if you tie the arms of your jacket around your waist and hold the two end corners up to catch the wind, you have a perfectly usable sail. Or take a sheet or blanket and a friend out to the pond. The friend holds two ends, you hold the other two—and together you really fly!

Ice Fishing

Once in a while, in the middle of the winter woods, I come upon a frozen lake dotted with ice fishermen—one here, one there, another a little farther out, yet another . . . Watching ice fishing—a few minutes at a time—is the closest I've ever come to it. In spite of the pleasure with which it has been described to me (and the pleasure I certainly take in the fish anyone cares to bring me), ice fishing remains one of the things I may never do. I doubt that I would ever have the kind of apparently infinite patience required to sit and wait for a fish to bite in subfreezing weather. To be sure, not all the people I see are just sitting and waiting. Some are moving from hole to hole, some are flat out on the ice peering into the depths through the hole, others are busy cutting new holes, some are hauling in vast quantities of fish. Nevertheless, it is not one of the most active of winter possibilities.

But it is one of the simplest. That is, beyond warm clothes, it requires very little gear. For panfish—small fish like perch, smelt, sunfish, bluegills, crappies—the most common catch for ice fishermen, you can get by with nothing more than a length of two-pound test transparent monofilament line, a small hook (panfish have small mouths), and a small split shot. Split shot is a kind of sinker that won't give much resistance to the fish (i.e., clue him in to the fact he is about to be caught) when he takes your bait. Buy a few. Sinkers get lost in water easily. Clamp the sinker on about a foot from the bottom of the line. Many ice fishermen use the line hand over hand, but if you prefer to use a rod and reel, the rod should be medium stiff and only about two and a half feet long. Your line should be lowered almost to the bottom since most of the action happens near there—from six inches to a foot and a half off the bottom. Fish are too sluggish in winter to put much effort into going after your bait, so you have to get it close to them. Fish don't even eat much in winter, so your bait should also be especially tasty. A local tackle shop can tell you what will most tempt the local fish.

When a fish finally does bite, it is often hard to detect it. You have to be alert to the smallest movement (*that* part appeals to me—if only it weren't so damn cold . . .) or invest in a tip-up, a simple device that waves a flag when you've hooked a fish. This is a fairly standard piece of equipment for ice fishermen who are tending more than one hole. You can easily make one— fasten a small flag (any piece of bright-colored cloth) to a stick a foot or two long; then tie this stick with a strong string at right angles to the center of a second stick. Leave a short piece of the flag stick projecting over the second stick, which must be long enough to span the hole, with a few inches left over on each side to rest on the ice. The flag stick also starts out lying down on the ice. The line and hook are attached to the short, projecting end of the flag stick and lowered through the hole. When a fish is hooked his movements will raise the flag.

You can purchase a slightly more sophisticated version, made of aluminum tubing, at tackle shops. With this rig you will need an underwater reel as well.

The hole itself can be cut with a chisel, an ice drill, or an auger, available at sporting goods stores or hardware stores. An ax makes a sloppy hole—which doesn't really matter except that you want the edges smooth so the line won't catch on them and fray and break at the exact moment you are bringing in the biggest fish ever caught in the lake. An ice spud, a long-handled implement designed for tapping and probing the ice ahead of you to make sure it is safe, can also be used to cut a hole, but the banging it makes will probably scare away any nearby fish. (For testing the ice, you don't need the ice spud. You can use the technique described in "Skating on a Woodland Pond." The ice should be about four inches thick.) Whatever you use to cut your holes, if you tie a rope around its handle and attach the rope to something solid (like you), it is less apt to slip out of your possibly icy glove—or somewhat numbed hand—and sink, irretrievably, to the bottom.

A hole five or six inches in diameter is usually adequate, with the bottom larger than the top. Snow and slush piled around the hole help block out light, but keep them out of the hole since, inside, they can speed up the formation of a new crust. Sport shops have a few contraptions to keep a new crust from forming, but you needn't worry about that if you keep the fish moving through the hole. Of course, you can keep them moving only if they are there to keep moving. Try to cut the hole where the fish are.

Reports on where fish are biting and ice is thick appear in local papers. The fish wardens of your state department of conservation or fish and game can also provide much of this information (plus information on fishing regulations and licenses). Local tackle shops can be helpful. So can, at times, bait dealers in the area and chambers of commerce, although they have a vested interest in your fishing in their area.

Wherever you are, the best fishing is early in the season, just after the lakes freeze, or very late, about the time the ice gets dangerous. At any time, a map of the lake bottom (available from state conservation or fish and game departments, local tackle shops or chambers of commerce) is helpful. The maps show the contour of the bottom, sand bars, drop-offs, weed beds, deep holes. Weeds, stumps, drop-offs, and so forth provide the cover smaller fish need to live and feed. Local maps are probably best because they often have the areas marked where you will—usually—find the most fish. Unless otherwise indicated, a drop-off shown on the map is a good place to begin. Cut the hole on its shore side.

With or without a map, notice where the other fishermen are. They will never be evenly spread over a lake, but more or less concentrated in what must be, for the moment, a hot spot—that magic place where the fish are finding oxygen, food, and cover . . . and your bait.

Give the fish about fifteen minutes to bite. If nothing

happens, move on to a new spot. Use the hole you've already cut to look underwater for weeds that could provide good cover. Lie down on the ice with your face next to the water and cover your head with a coat to cut out any reflection. Or use a waterscope or bottomless bucket or sponge bucket (see "Collecting Shells"). Where it looks likely, cut a new hole. Give that one fifteen minutes. Or try the abandoned hole of an earlier fisherman. However sluggish they may be, the fish do move around.

Ice fishing is cold. You must *keep* warm while you're fishing because for sure you won't *get* warm fishing. (Although I understand there was an enterprising lady in Minnesota who made some warming rounds of the Minnesota lakes in a blacked-out station wagon. But then, that's a local event.)

One of the most important pieces of clothing is a wool or fur hat that also covers your ears. (Heat goes out through your head.) Many fishermen wear one-piece coveralls. Down ski warm-ups will do nicely too, or various combinations of layers of wool, the bottom of which should be long underwear. Two pairs of wool socks and felt boot liners (available at sporting goods shops—deer hunters wear them) inside high rubber boots are essential. Ice is not only cold, but wet. When a hole is cut, water comes up. When the sun comes out, water appears. The boots should be kept loose both for good (warming) circulation and so you can kick them off if you fall through the ice. Take two pairs of gloves because one pair will always be wet. Pin or clip them on a string around your neck—as your mother did for you when you were four—so you can get them out of your way when working or keep them from falling into the hole. Add a pair of cotton work gloves to make cleaning the fish on the ice bearable.

Carry a compass. In case of a white-out you could become totally disoriented, even on a small lake where you are not far from shore. To guard against this— *before* the white-out—take a reading from your starting point to your fishing site so you can reverse your route to return. Keep track of how long it took you to get to your site from the start so you'll know how long it *should* take to get back.

In some places fishermen erect little shacks, and whole lakes look like arctic shanty towns. Many fishermen use easily portable, pop-up tents. Some simply rig a windbreak with a tarp or a piece of plywood or canvas. A heater is not a bad idea, nor is a handwarmer or two slipped into your pockets, and hot lunch in a thermos is a virtual necessity. A small stove, like those backpackers carry, provides a way to make hot chocolate, coffee, or soup quickly and easily. This could serve to warm you more than just internally if, for instance, you have a neighbor on the ice who seems to be catching a lot of fish while you're not. The offer of a cup of something hot may improve *your* fishing no end.

Ice Fishing, Jerry Chiapetta, Stackpole Books, Harrisburg, Pa., 1975. Thorough and easy to read. Hardcover.

New Fisherman's Encyclopedia, Ira N. Gabrielson, editor, Stackpole Books, Harrisburg, Pa., 1977. This is of use to all fishermen, not just those on ice. Hardcover.

Going for a Walk

Winter is a great gift of open space. With the trees bare, whole new landscapes, hidden by summer's green, emerge. I feel as if the forests of other seasons in my region have given way to the high, alpine landscape I love. I am no longer enclosed and sheltered by the all-enveloping green but find, instead, that even the most gentle woods are full of the wild beauty of the most rugged backcountry. Winter is a time to feel adventure, without having to go to much trouble—beyond dressing properly—to do it.

Where the land is even and the snow not deep, a winter walk is easy and uncomplicated. I simply throw on a few layers of clothes (which include long underwear, two pairs of warm wool socks, and waterproof boots), grab a wool hat and mittens, and fill a thermos with something hot to warm the stops I make to look at views. Since there are lots of views in winter I carry quite a large thermos.

Even on the coldest day you will get warm as you walk, so it is essential to dress in a way that allows for the removing of outer clothes along the way. You can put them quickly back on when you stop, *before* you cool off . . .

If the day is a snowy one when you can easily become disoriented, make sure there is something specific to follow—a canal, a road, trail markers on trees. Or be expert enough with a compass to use it even if you get cold and disoriented and find yourself in the middle of a snowstorm. In winter, even the clearest day can suddenly become snowy. One of the nicest walks I ever had happened specifically *because* I got disoriented. Of course, it was in a safe place—New York City's Central Park—where I had the security of knowing I couldn't really get lost.

The surrounding buildings utterly disappeared in a white-out. I lost track of my direction. There was nothing but snow—everywhere. White snow, white ground, white sky. Not a sign of people. No cars. No buildings, dogs, police—nothing. For hours, nothing. Me and an uninhabited, untracked wilderness. It was an utterly private time.

(It was also safe. Muggers rarely go out for walks in a snowstorm.)

Cross-Country Skiing

The meadows behind the house seemed to me a perfect place to ski, but my friends knew a better place. Everything, I guess, is relative. They live there all the time, and I had come out from the city.

We skied down a snow-covered dirt road and came to an area of rolling hills that stretched back and farther back, as far as we could see, gentle, open, here and there defined by a low stone wall, occasionally punctuated by a stand of trees. We started on level ground, then, almost without realizing it, found ourselves climbing. The far side of the hill was steeper and we ran straight down, aiming for an opening in a stone wall. It was a wide enough opening to allow for a slight lapse of aim.

The temperature was in the twenties, but the sun was brilliant and we quickly became warm. New snow had fallen the day before, then, overnight, had blown and hardened into a fast, sometimes crusty surface, untracked and endless. We traversed, climbed, ran down, fell now and then, glided easily along the level sections, and stopped, finally, for lunch.

Cross-country skiing makes you warm. There's hardly a muscle in your body that isn't being used. The result may be the loosest-looking glide you ever saw, but everything's working to make it happen. So you need very few clothes while skiing. And a lot of clothes for lunch. We put on down parkas and wool hats and arranged the skis into benches to keep us off the snow. (Three skis, placed bindings-down, make a good bench. If you carry a small piece of ensolite—available in backpacking stores—to place on top as a cushion, you have some elegant moisture-proof seating. Make sure all the snow is out of the bindings when you are ready to ski again.) We leaned back against a stone wall hit full by the sun and settled down to the lunch of wine, cheese, fruit, and freshly baked bread we had packed in our rucksacks. (Skiers—cross-country and downhill—have a better sense of lunch than anybody else I've ever met. If I didn't ski, I'd still like to lunch with skiers.)

It was a simple afternoon: a short ski run, a lovely lunch, virgin snow, the glory of the winter sun on the hills and on us. There was a purity and an ease in the day and in the actual physical communion with the landscape. Every movement on skis is made in direct contact with the winter earth; ease and effort are physically connected to the contours of the earth. Because it happens faster than walking, contact with the earth is more intense. Your body reacts, your mind follows. Only when your body stops, does your mind question—is this too steep to run straight? Is that gate too narrow? That slope too icy? Keep moving and you keep moving.

It is a cliché to say that anyone who can walk can cross-country ski. But, of course, it is true. The movement is different—rather than step you thrust forward and glide—but unlike the movement of downhill skiing, it is a natural movement, providing a natural way to explore the outdoors in winter. Natural, but strenuous since, as I mentioned earlier, virtually every muscle, including your heart, is used. If you regularly ride a bicycle, play tennis or golf, swim, jog, hike, or do another sport or some sort of physical labor, you won't find it overly strenuous. If not, you might consider gentle winter walks instead (same possibilities for lunch, after all), until you get yourself into slightly better shape.

To try cross-country skiing, borrow or rent skis, boots, and poles at the first sign of a good snowfall. (If the skis require waxing, get waxing instructions—and wax—from their owner or at the shop.) Then spend a few hours learning the uncomplicated basics, either from a proficient friend (*you* bring the lunch) or from a professional. If the shop where you rent equipment is in the city, ask about the nearest place to go for instruction. If the shop is at a cross-country ski center or in traditional ski country, they may offer instruction themselves.

Then go off for fun. Move at your own pace. Ski with people of your own ability. (If you are a novice, it could be the end of pleasure, rather than the beginning, to make a tour with experts with whom you cannot possibly keep up.) Start out easily—a two-hour tour, lunch, and two hours back is plenty. Less is OK too. Longer distances over more varied terrain will come on their own.

Cross-country ski centers, with marked trails, have sprung up everywhere in snow country. They supply maps of their areas, including the marked trails. If you are skiing *off* the trails, be sure you have a map— and an awareness that the closer together the contours are, the steeper the terrain. If there are shelters where you can stop (sometimes with stoves on which you can cook a hot lunch), they will also be marked on the map.

But you are not limited to official ski centers. Golf courses, bridle paths unused in winter, country roads, city parks, meadows, fields, canal towpaths, abandoned railroad rights-of-way—you can ski anywhere. New York City parks seem actually to breed skiers through a kind of spontaneous generation after a new snow.

The possibility of skiing anywhere is one of the advantages cross-country skiers have over downhill skiers. There are others. Cross-country skiers need less snow; they are not dependent on mechanical devices to get to the top of the mountain; they are not surrounded by hordes of other skiers—and they don't have to spend anything at all, beyond the initial (generally reasonable) investment in equipment.

These factors also explain the recent renaissance of this ancient activity. Sharing its origins with snowshoeing, it is a method of transportation thousands of years old. In some parts of the world it still is a means of transportation. One February, while driving a snow-covered back road above the Arctic Circle, I came upon an aged Lapp on skis. I imagined he was on his way from one settlement to the next. I stopped the car on the road side—not to watch, but because I felt the car, the motor, was an anomaly. I wanted it—and me—not to be there. In the world through which he moved there were only the sounds of nature and the faint swish of his skis. I suppose, in a way, I wasn't there. He never turned to look at me but continued straight ahead as he had done for centuries.

I am never on skis now but that I think of him.

The Complete Guide to Cross-Country Skiing and Touring, Art Tokle and Martin Luray, Vintage, New York, 1973. A complete guide and superb introduction to technique and equipment. Mr. Tokle is a member of the Ski Hall of Fame, member of the U.S. Nordic team, and coach of the U.S. jumping team. Mr. Luray has been editorial director of *Skiing Magazine* and *Ski Magazine.* Paper. Also available in French.

The New Cross-Country Ski Book, John Caldwell, Stephen Greene Press, Brattleboro, Vt. 05301, 1976. Another good guide and introduction to technique and equipment by another former Olympic skier and U.S. team coach. Paper.

Ski Touring: An Introductory Guide, William E. Osgood and Leslie J. Hurley, Charles E. Tuttle Co., 28 S. Main St., Rutland, Vt. 05701, 1969. Same spirit as their snowshoe book.

Wilderness Skiing, Lito Tesada-Flores and Allen Steck, Sierra Club Totebook (see *Associations*), 1972. This one goes off into the realm of alpine touring and ski mountaineering. Everything you need to know—once you know how to ski—is in it.

Ski Touring Guide covers the basic touring areas in the eastern United States. $2.00 from the Ski Touring Council (see *Associations*).

Associations

The Ski Touring Council is a nonprofit organization devoted to encouraging ski touring as recreation. They sponsor touring clinics, workshops, and tours in New England, New York, New Jersey, and Pennsylvania— free except for a registration charge. Their annual schedule, which includes information on where instruction is offered, costs $2.50. For more information write: Rudolf F. Mattesich, Ski Touring Council, West Hill Road, Troy, Vt. 05868.

United States Ski Association is the major skiing organization in the United States. Its Nordic Committee sponsors ski touring clinics, including ski mountaineering instruction. For more information write: Nordic Committee, United States Ski Association, 1726 Champa Street, Suite 300, Denver, Colo. 80202.

The Sierra Club sponsors ski touring and ski mountaineering outings. For information about the ski activities of the chapter nearest you write: Winter Sports Committee, Sierra Club, 530 Bush Street, San Francisco, Calif. 94108.

Many outdoor or mountain clubs sponsor ski touring outings. Contact one in your area—if there happens to be snow in your area. See the list following "A Walk in the Woods."

Commercial Outfitters

There are commercial outfitters who conduct guided tours through gentle wilderness and the wildest mountains. Tours are standard or custom-made and many outfitters rent equipment. A state-by-state listing is to be found in *Adventure Travel USA,* available for $3.50 from Adventure Trip Guide, Inc., 36 E. 57th St., New York, N.Y. 10022. A few are listed in *Explorer's Ltd. Source Book,* edited by Alwin T. Perrin, Harper & Row, New York, 1973.

Ski Orienteering

Ski orienteering is a way of adding a little extra spice to cross-country skiing without having to increase the difficulty of the skiing. It can be done on the easiest of ski trails by someone who is both relatively inexperienced as a skier and totally inexperienced as an orienteer.

Like orienteering on foot (see "Fall"), it can be a competitive sport but doesn't have to be, although as a competitive sport it is actually older than orienteering on foot.

The chief difference between the two is a difference in the kind of terrain chosen for the course. On foot, you want the route to make its way through a landscape with a variety of natural features—hills, streams, mountains, meadows—seemingly untracked terrain through which the orienteer must find his own way.

But the ski orienteer, skiing over untracked terrain, leaves tracks to advertise where he has gone. The next orienteer to arrive in the area cannot possibly ignore the tracks a pair of skis make over an otherwise pristine hill.

To remedy this, the control points must be located so that there is a variety of route choices along snow-covered roads and ski trails. By using existing cross-country tracks or trails, the skier can avoid making new tracks and displaying his route to other skiers.

A popular form of ski orienteering is point orienteering, probably the easiest form of course to set up. The skier follows a ski touring course already marked on his map. The trail selected should be one that passes through as many fixed points as possible—trail junctions, hilltops, frozen lakes—any features that will make it easy for the participant continually to reconfirm his position on the map. He should do this often in preparation for marking, on his map, the precise location of each control. The "winner" is the person with the most accurate marking of the most controls on his map. This simply amounts to knowing, at every moment, exactly where you are on the map—which is, after all, the essence of orienteering.

Since all of this is done on a marked and maintained ski trail, it is ideal for inexperienced orienteers. There is no possible way to get lost so long as you stay on the trail. It is also superb practice for honing your compass and map-reading skills.

If you cover the course alone—even the simplest course—ski orienteering provides an impression of serious adventure, in spite of the other ski tracks on the trail. After all, it's just you, your compass, map, and trusty old skis conquering the cold, racing across the windswept countryside, traversing a wilderness where only your own skill keeps you fully aware of where you are . . .

Not only that, but it's fun.

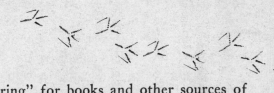

See "Orienteering" for books and other sources of information.

Night

Stars are falling, fish jumping, coyotes howling, bob-cat hunting. Night-blooming cereus is in flower and a hundred birds are flying across the moon. Crabs are mating, shrimp are biting, snow is sparkling, lizards, snakes, and Gila monsters are making their nightly rounds of the life-teeming desert.

Night has its own seasons. Ruled by the moon, it is a magical world offering union with mystery to all who enter. It is a secret time, to be entered softly, slipped into with the silence of the wildcat, observed with the patience of the wolf.

The Night Sky

We had the sky up there, all speckled with stars, and we used to lay on our backs and look up at them, and discuss about whether they was made or just happened. Jim said the moon could 'a' laid them; well, that looked kind of reasonable, so I didn't say nothing against it, because I've seen a frog lay most as many, so of course, it could be done. We used to watch the stars that fell, too, and see them streak down. Jim allowed they'd got spoiled and was hove out of the nest.

— Huckleberry Finn

I lay on my back one night in a vast, high meadow in Wyoming. It was a moonless night, clear and black, glittering with stars piled on stars and pierced by the far-off cry of a coyote—farther away than any stars. Staring at the stars I felt lifted, pulled up into the dome of the sky, into that teeming cold brilliance. The Milky Way stretched across heaven, a hundred thousand million stars shimmering. The brightest stars stood out from the great mass like jewels on a dress of jewels. Occasional dark patches, dust clouds, looming mysterious like black holes in the sky, hid the stars beneath them.

It was a warm night and I lay on top of my sleeping bag instead of inside. I thought of all the years of summer nights when, going outside for air and coolness, I found myself under a sky full of stars. I would just sit and watch, picking out those few stars and constellations I know, recognizing a planet here and there.

Stars can be as familiar as a much-traveled path in the woods; read as easily as an oft-used map; identified, discovered wherever in the sky they are. One needn't know all their names, or even very many (or quite possibly, any) to feel them as familiars. (Can something that twinkles be unfriendly?)

But it's a nice feeling, going out after dark and looking up to recognize a few old friends. It makes a solitary night walk less so. You are, wherever you are, in familiar territory. A New Yorker who finds himself suddenly transported to Utah, possibly awed and baffled by the landscape, need only look up to see familiar territory. That is, if he's ever looked up in New York.

There *are* stars in New York. And in other cities too, in spite of city lights and reports to the contrary. People in cities can see at least first- and second-magnitude stars.

Magnitude is the measure of a star's or planet's brightness. The lower the number, the brighter the star. There are twenty-one first-magnitude stars in our galaxy, although some are visible only in the Southern Hemisphere. A star is always the same brightness; a planet changes brightness. But both stars and planets *seem* dimmer when they are close to the horizon where their light has a longer path through the earth's absorbing atmosphere. Under ideal conditions—when your eyes are fully adapted to the dark, the sky is clear, there is no moon and no glow from city lights— you may just be able to see stars up to the fifth magnitude.

Like the sun, stars rise in the east and set in the west. That is, the stars (like the sun) stay where they are, and where we see them depends on the position of the earth as it spins on its axis and revolves around the sun. If you see a star in one part of the sky one night, a few nights later you will find it in another. Or you may see it in the same spot, but earlier, or later. The constellations change too, tilting in various, progressive positions as they make their nightly trip across the sky. (That is, as *we* make the trip.)

If you have nothing else to do one night, you might like to spend it watching the Big Dipper. Starting out in a position to hold water, it will move to stand on its handle, then to spill water on the North Star (Polaris), and, finally, to hang from its handle before returning to its original position. The North Star, meanwhile, is always in the same relation to it—just about in line with the two stars (called the Pointers) that form the side of the Dipper away from the handle.

The Big Dipper is not a constellation, but an asterism, which is simply a part of a constellation—in this case, Ursa Major. The Pointers are an asterism within the asterism of the Big Dipper.

The North Star, Kochab (a star almost as bright as

the North Star), and a few dimmer stars form the Little Dipper. Kochab lies between the North Star and the Big Dipper's handle. On the side of the Little Dipper, *opposite* the Big Dipper, is Cassiopeia, whose five stars are about as bright as the North Star and Kochab—all second-magnitude stars. There are no brighter stars (that is, first-magnitude stars) and no planets next to the North Star.

Cassiopeia is a queen sitting in a chair. You may be able to envision the chair. The queen is another matter. What it actually looks like is a kind of casual letter M when above the North Star and an equally casual W when below it.

The North Star always indicates north—should you get lost while stargazing. North of the fortieth degree north latitude (southern Pennsylvania to northern California) you can easily find it just by finding the Big Dipper. If you're south of that latitude, however, parts of the Big Dipper sink below the horizon in certain positions. Starting at about mid-Florida, the Big Dipper will be entirely below the horizon when it is directly below the North Star (in the position to hold water). But all is not lost. Use Cassiopeia. At those times when the Big Dipper is wholly or partly invisible, Cassiopeia will be an M high in the sky, with one end of the M pointing to the North Star.

But pick your own star. Watch its progress through the sky from month to month, season to season. Since it follows precisely the same route every year, you will be able—after a year of watching—to use it as a calendar. You needn't even know its name. "Mine," you simply call it.

SPECIAL EVENTS IN THE SKY

Shooting stars—meteors—are bits of matter, once probably part of a comet, that heat up and glow when they enter the earth's atmosphere. Most quickly burn themselves out, but occasionally one explodes as a fire-ball with fantastic effect that can be seen for hundreds of miles. Some shooting stars—meteorites—are fragments of asteroids. These can range in size from an ounce or less to sixty tons or more and often reach the earth without being entirely vaporized. Before recorded history a number of giant meteorites fell with force enough to scoop out immense craters. There are two verified meteorite craters in the United States. Canyon Diablo in Arizona is 4,660 feet in diameter and over 626 feet deep. Odessa in Texas is more than 582 feet in diameter and 198 feet deep.

Most shooting stars occur after midnight. The last hours of a moonless night often produce whole showers of them. More or less reliable, annual showers not only allow you to make plans for a meteor viewing, but provide you with a choice of seasons. Meteor showers extend over a period of days, with activity usually peaking on a specific day. Check your local paper, natural history museum, or the astronomy department of a local university for the peak day. Approximate dates are: April 20, May 5, July 20, August 11 (meteors appearing on this day—the Perseids—are the most spectacular), October 20, November 16, and December 13. Settle yourself in a comfortable spot; take insect repellent in the warm seasons, warm clothes at most seasons, and a little patience. You may see two or three within seconds, then no more for several minutes.

Don't forget that shooting stars are for wishing.

Comets are something else. Rarer. About every ten years one is visible to the unaided eye. Comets consist of loose rocks (from the size of dust to the size of boulders) and frozen gasses. They orbit around the sun, coming near it (where we can see them) on regular schedules that vary from once every few years to once in thousands of years. The best-known comet—Halley's comet—appears every seventy-six years. All its appearances have been traced back as far as the third century b.c. It's due back in 1986.

Of all the lights of night, no other has quite the effect—on me, at least—of the Northern Lights. The first time I saw them I was camped on a lakeshore in Ontario's Algonquin Park during a canoe trip. Suddenly, high up over the dark forest on the opposite side of the lake, there appeared a kind of shimmery greenish light, hanging like curtains in midair, immense and terrifying. Other colors entered; the glow increased in intensity in waves, pulsating. "Northern Lights," someone said. In that timorous, formidable, yet accepting instant before I knew what I was seeing, I felt possessed by the vision. Now I could not take my eyes from it. No one could.

Luminous, awesome, Aurora Borealis—the Northern Lights—forms streamers, arcs, draperies, or banks of yellow, green, blue, and violet. It appears most often along a line extending from mid-Hudson Bay through Point Barrow, Alaska. Seeing it is rare in the lower states, although it does, on occasion, come farther south. Friends of mine have seen it in New York State and Vermont. It occurs most often at the time of the equinoxes and seems to coincide with times of the greatest sunspot activity and magnetic storms—disturbances of part of the upper atmosphere that interfere with long-distance radio communication. In other words, if your CB radio is out of whack, and you live reasonably far north, and it's the first day of spring or fall, this is a superb opportunity for you to engage in the simple pleasure of going out to some dark hill for a look at the sky and perhaps the experience of the Northern Lights.

It has nothing to do with things of the Earth.

The Night Earth

Several times in the Alps I have started off late to hike to a mountain hut and found myself overtaken by night. But there, above tree line where the rock reflects its full measure of moon or starlight, where the sky itself seems less densely black, walking at night is easy. The *feeling* of walking is different from the feeling of walking during the day, but in clear weather the path is no more difficult to see, and I walk along at the same pace I use during the day.

But when I deliberately set out to make a nighttime walk, it becomes an event full of mystery. I move slowly—or possibly not at all. (Can one call not moving a "walk"?) This kind of "walk" provides a perfect opportunity for an outdoor adventure to people who don't want to move much. The less you move, in fact, the more you will see. And if you allow your eyes time to adjust to the dark, you will see well— almost as well as owls or lynx and better than bears. (In case you're nervous about bears, that means *you* will see *them* first.) It takes about fifteen minutes for the iris to widen to its furthest extent, where it can capture most of whatever natural light is available—stars; moon; water, snow, sand, or rock reflecting stars and/or moon. In less than an hour the retina has adjusted and can make full use of the iris. Start your night walk by just sitting for three quarters of an hour, until your eyes are fully adjusted. Your backyard is fine, but cut out all artificial light.

Or, if it makes you too uneasy to go without *some* light, use a red light (red-covered or painted flashlight or headlamp). Most nocturnal animals do not see red light. If the light is attached to your head—like a miner's lamp—your hands are free for binoculars, or anything else.

Watch everywhere. Listen. You will hear sounds first. Then something will come by. It may walk or crawl, slither or fly; it may just suddenly appear in the branch of a tree. Witness—you have become a part of the night.

THE BEACH

I am perfecting not-moving while writing this book when, at night, I go to sit on the beach. Just before it is entirely dark I am privy to the tremendous activity taking place around the houses of the tens of thousands of sand fleas. And the crabs are out with a vengeance. Just there, a horseshoe crab—great, horny, ugly thing that he is—sidles into the ocean. The ghost crabs (sand crabs) come out of their burrows and walk down to the water's edge, wait for a wave to wash in and wet their bodies, then rush back to drier beach to eat before

returning to the safety of their burrows toward dawn.
(If they dawdle a bit on their way they stand a good
chance of being eaten by a gull. I saw a rather errant
crab captured by a gull in midafternoon the other day.
The gull snatched the crab off the sand, then walked
across the beach toward the dunes with the crab's legs
hanging, wriggling out of his mouth. A young gull
followed, begging for a bit of lunch, but the adult
ignored him, flew off a short distance, landed, and continued walking across the beach. The young one remained where he was but walked in circles, crying.)

I have yet to catch sight of a sea turtle. They come
up onto the sand at night to select a site for their
eggs . . . beyond the reach of the waves, but within
sight of them. Here they prepare a deep pit, lay from
fifty to two hundred eggs, push sand in to hide the
nest, then head back to sea. About seven weeks later
the young turtles emerge, usually also at night.

As I sit, the moon comes up, full and glowing,
orange at first and then white. Moonglow streaks the
water. The whitecaps seem phosphorescent. I can
match their glow by scraping my toes or fingers in the
damp sand next to the sea to uncover millions of
diatoms—minuscule phosphorescent animals. The sand
is alive and sparkling with them.

THE FOREST

A night walk through woods—even the most familiar
woods—seems more mysterious (although less exotic)
than being on the beach. I feel a certain caution; ap-
prehension almost. What was that sound? And that?

That movement over there? That shadow? That spark of light, here and gone? Voices and eyes of night are on every side of me; wind and cloud combine in ghostly movement to touch me as they pass; the eyes of a fox glow in the clearing; a deer, its great hulk dark and double the size of morning, bounds across the dirt road, crashes into the woods, and is gone; an owl hoots, night hunter, his cry more wild than the cry of any wolf or coyote, more lonely than any loon; his cry the essence of night.

Night is different from day. I think that's less simple than it sounds. People are beings of light, of day. Whatever our social preferences, night is not our natural time. A little awe, a little hesitation, are natural. The more we know about the life of night, the less frightening it is, of course. But it always remains that night is a foreign time.

Night exaggerates sound. You can hear the dew dripping from leaf to leaf, or the scratching sounds made in dry leaves by a beetle. (These may be exaggerated enough to convince you they are being made by a bear. Try to identify where the sound is coming from and look over there. If the sound continues and you don't see a bear, it's probably a beetle.)

Once, lying in my tent around midnight, I heard a crashing in the bushes a few feet away, a heavy crashing, such as deer or moose make. It was followed by silence, then a kind of chomping of leaves, and finally by a series of low moans. A moose with a stomachache, I reasoned. I looked out of the tent and, sure enough, there, close enough to touch, hulking black against the moonless night, was a moose. With or without a stomachache. At the time I thought it would be nice if it were a beetle.

But not in retrospect. In retrospect it was quite extraordinary. What I mean to say is, some large sounds do, in fact, belong to large animals. Don't be alarmed by exaggerated sounds, but don't automatically dismiss them as night exaggerations. You might miss seeing some wonderful creatures.

The animals you will see are not interested in you. They are hunting, or chasing, or eating whatever it is they ordinarily eat. They do this at night because they are safer then from whatever preys on them. Many of them are also physically more comfortable in cool night air. You have more chance of seeing them then than you ever would during the day, in suburban areas and city parks as well as in the woods. Flying squirrels, the most nocturnal of mammals, for instance, are not uncommon in city parks.

Out of curiosity some animals might check you out, then leave you alone. Most will just run away. If, however, you stay utterly still, they will probably return to the spot where they were hunting, fishing, or eating.

Rub yourself and your clothes with a scent natural to an animal—like balsam, honeysuckle, or sagebrush —to disguise the human scent and you will have an even greater chance to observe. You can increase your *own* sense of smell by wetting your nose. You may have noticed sometime that all smells are sharper on a damp night.

Moisture magnifies smells the way night magnifies sound. The senses become bigger than life. Or perhaps just big enough to encompass it.

THINGS THAT GLOW IN THE NIGHT

There are many things that glow besides the tiny beach creatures I mentioned earlier. One of the most spectacular of night phenomena happens in suburban backyards, among other places. Fireflies. I still love to catch them—for an instant—long enough to see the light in my cupped palms and then to let it go, quite pleased with myself for being able to tell the difference between a male and a female. (The difference is apparent, for me, from where they are, not how they look. Males flash their lights while flying above females who stay on the ground and answer by flashing their own lights.)

Those tiny dots of light in a row on the ground—glowworms—are firefly larvae. Bits of light glowing in rotten logs are beetle grubs. Rotten logs can also be host to the ghostly glow of slime fungus, a plant that creeps—glowing—over the logs or along the ground. Eerie. Unearthly. Sometimes you might see an animal, a bear or raccoon, whose front paws glow in the dark. He is not a ghost. He has simply been rooting around in one of these logs.

Other lights you are apt to see are eyes of animals—gleaming points of red, orange, yellow, or white; the flash of water disturbed by an animal fishing; the swift flame of silver as a fish jumps for insects in the moonlight.

Winter Night

Glittering, brilliant, crumbled diamonds of snow catch and reflect moon and starlight, sparkle like the stars themselves. But the stars are up to it. Every bit a match for the snow-covered hills and valleys is the Milky Way, more dense than ever, impenetrably white.

Where the dark shapes of evergreens stand eternal guard on the flanks of luminescent mountains, winter night is my favorite season. The only sound is the crunch of snow underfoot. The world becomes pure, inviolate. No one has touched it. No one else has ever been there.

A Field Guide to the Stars and Planets, Donald H. Menzel, Houghton Mifflin Co., Boston, 1964. Hardcover and paper.

How to Read the Night Sky, W. S. Kals, Doubleday & Co., New York, 1974. Hardcover.

Knowing the Outdoors in the Dark, Vinson Brown, Collier Books, New York, 1973. Paper.

The World of Night, Lorus J. Milne and Margery J. Milne, Harper & Brothers, New York. A superb guidebook to the night.

Natural History is the publication of the American Museum of Natural History in New York City. Every issue contains a star map and a discussion of current celestial events. It is published monthly October through May, bimonthly June to September. $10.00 a year. Write: Natural History, Membership Services, Box 6000, Des Moines, Iowa 50340. Subscription price includes membership in the Museum.

Appendixes

It is a vulgar error to suppose that you have tasted huckleberries who never plucked them.

—Thoreau

National Recreation Areas

All is not wilderness in urban national parks. Part of the function of the National Park Service is to protect historical sites within these areas. And there is, of course, as there is bound to be in urban areas, the dispute over whether parks should be geared toward recreational facilities—baseball diamonds, swimming pools, and parking lots—or toward maintaining whatever wild character they still have. Final resolutions will lie with the users, both of parks that already exist and of those that—we hope—will be created.

Golden Gate National Recreation Area, California, consists of more than 35,000 acres. Its northwest boundary abuts Point Reyes National Seashore, and together the two areas comprise over 100,000 acres, accessible from San Francisco. The Municipal Railway bus system serves many of the San Francisco parts of the park, while Golden Gate Transit serves the areas in Marin County—Muir Woods and Point Reyes National Seashore among them.

For more information write: Superintendent, Golden Gate National Recreation Area, Fort Mason, San Francisco, Calif. 94123.

Cuyahoga Valley National Recreation Area, Ohio, consists of about 30,000 acres extending about twenty miles along the Cuyahoga River from the southern edge of Cleveland to the northern edge of Akron. The old Ohio and Erie Canal ran through the region, and the towpath is still there to walk. One proof of the effectiveness of urban parks exists here. Since the park came into being, the beavers have come back to the river. The B&O Railroad runs an excursion train from downtown Cleveland into part of the park, but service needs to be expanded and shuttle buses added.

For more information write: Superintendent Cuyahoga Valley National Recreation Area, P.O. Box 158, Peninsula, Ohio 44264.

Indiana Dunes National Lakeshore, Indiana, was the country's first urban national park. It consists of about 8000 acres of sand dunes along Lake Michigan, sixty miles east of Chicago and exactly between Gary and Michigan City—that is, smack in the middle of one of the most industrial sections of the United States. Nearby there are steel mills, railways, highways, a large port—and the threat of a nuclear power plant— which make this some *very* special land. The Chicago South Shore and South Bend Railroad provides commuter service between Chicago and South Bend, with a number of stops in and near the Lakeshore.

For more information write: Superintendent, Indiana Dunes National Lakeshore, RR 2, Box 139 A, Chesterton, Ind. 46304.

Gateway National Recreation Area consists of 26,000 acres of parkland—in unconnected pieces—surrounding the entrance to New York Harbor. They have been divided into four units: Jamaica Bay, Breezy Point, Staten Island, and Sandy Hook (which is in New Jersey). Over 300 species of birds, migratory and resident, find their way to the Jamaica Bay Wildlife Refuge. People can reach it by subway.

For more information write: Superintendent, Gateway National Recreation Area, Headquarters Building 69, Floyd Bennett Field, Brooklyn, N.Y. 11234

Urban national parks either already are, or have the potential to be, the most intensively used parts of the National Park System. Transportation remains one of their biggest problems. The lack of public transportation encourages the use of private cars, which causes pressure for parking lots and roadways, an unfortunate use of limited and precious land. Wouldn't it be nicer, after all, to come upon a field of wildflowers than a parking lot? The dependence on private cars also cuts out a lot of people—among them, the elderly, teenagers, and many who live in the inner cities.

Among the arguments *against* better public transportation is one to the effect that it will bring in too many people. Maybe. But too many people without cars have a lot less impact than too many people with cars. Which is what it finally comes down to.

National Recreation Trails

The National Trails Systems Act authorized three kinds of trails: National Recreation Trails in or near urban areas; National Scenic Trails—like the 2000-mile Appalachian Trail from Maine to Georgia and the 2600-mile Pacific Crest Trail from Canada to Mexico; and connecting and side trails. Recreation Trails can be designated by the Secretary of the Interior and the Secretary of Agriculture. So far the Secretary of the Interior has designated twenty-nine trails in nineteen states and the District of Columbia. They range in length from just under 1200 feet to thirty miles and offer possibilities for walkers, hikers, bikers, horseback riders, and nature enthusiasts of all kinds. One trail, the quarter-mile-long Long Creek Trail in Kentucky, is designed to be usable by people confined to wheelchairs.

Information about these trails and other outdoor recreation is available from the seven regional offices of the U.S. Department of the Interior, Bureau of Outdoor Recreation. Write to the Regional Director:

Northwest Region, United Pacific Building, 1000 Second Avenue, Seattle, Wash. 98104

Pacific Southwest Region, Box 36062, 450 Golden Gate Avenue, San Francisco, Calif. 94102

Mid-Continent Region, Building 41, P.O. Box 25387, Denver Federal Center, Denver, Colo. 80225

Lake Central Region, 3853 Research Park Drive, Ann Arbor, Mich. 48104

Southeast Region, 148 Cain Street, Atlanta, Ga. 30303

Northeast Region, Federal Office Building, Rm. 9510, 600 Arch Street, Philadelphia, Pa. 19106

South Central Region, 5000 Marble Avenue, N.E., Albuquerque, N.Mex. 87110.